BAKING
COOKBOOK

Good Cook's Library

BAKING
COOKBOOK

Crescent Books
New York

© 1988 Ottenheimer Publishers, Inc.
This 1988 edition published by
Crescent Books, by arrangement with
Ottenheimer Publishers, Inc.,
distributed by Crown Publishers, Inc.,
225 Park Avenue South, New York, New York 10003

Printed and bound in Spain

ISBN 0-517-66210-8
h g f e d c b a

Contents

Useful Facts About Grain

Foreword

"Natural Baking" means exactly what it says—baking using only the best natural ingredients and wholewheat flour whenever possible. These make a spicier and more appetizing healthy food than ordinary baking using refined and adulterated products, such as white flour. Why not try it out for yourself with this new illustrated cookbook? It will both delight and surprise you.

Whole Grain Baking

Baking with whole grain and natural ingredients enables you to keep to a high fiber diet and also enjoy deliciously flavored food. This is especially true of rolls, bread and dessert pastries which your family will soon insist on as part of their regular meals. Cakes and confectionery will also be more nutritious, allowing you to eat more snacks without ruining your diet. This is why wholemeal rather than white flour is used in these recipes. Different flours have been combined where possible. This balances the vital nutritive properties of baking with the appetizing smell of freshly baked food. The use of refined sugar is purposely restricted to decoration, and practically no artificial flavoring is used. Almond extract, for instance, is never needed as tests show that natural spices, nuts and seeds, produce exactly the same effect.

Nutritional Value

Unfortunately wholemeal flour baking does not produce a lower calorie level than refined flour or sugar (calories are stated in each recipe). But among the many advantages of wholemeal products is that you tend to eat less of them even though they are tastier. Also you will find that they stop you from feeling hungry for longer periods. The nutritional value of protein, fat, carbohydrates and the more important fibers have also been added to each recipe.

The Ingredients

Most of the ingredients listed can be bought in large supermarkets and health food shops without difficulty, although seasonal availability of fresh fruits, nuts, etc. have to be taken into account. If you live in a small town or an area with limited shopping facilities, your baker or pharmacist may be able to get some ingredients for you.

Attractive Recipes

The recipes for this book have been created to be used in a normal household with standard kitchen equipment. All the recipes have been tested and the photographs genuinely show the results of the baking. Just leafing through the book should wet both your interest and appetite, and hopefully, make you want to try out the dishes as soon as possible. As the titles show, most of the recipes are for familiar dishes, including spicy ring-cakes and fancy shortbreads, butter cream cakes, Christmas fruitbread, pear cake with walnuts, plum cake with hazelnuts, and sesame and pretzels, as well as, marzipan confectionary, rye rolls, mixed grain bread, leek and onion flan, and tomato pizza. The cooking method is presented in "work" order and in as detailed, simple to follow, and easy way as possible. Hopefully, this new approach of mixing rediscovered and traditional ingredients will give you the confidence to produce first class, attractive and appetizing baking.

Shopping Tips

First, a word about whole grain. Only buy it from a good quality supplier, like a health food shop.
If you want to try grinding your own grain there are mills on the market, some as attachments for standard kitchen grinders and blenders.
Spices should be ground in with the grain to ensure a good aromatic blend. Thus it is better not to buy pre-ground spices as their flavor tends to fade too quickly.

Baking Methods

Each recipe has been carefully detailed so that even the most inexperienced home baker should find them straightforward. However, additional information is contained in the chapter on grain types and their specific baking characteristics. Keen amateur cooks should have no trouble as the actual method of making dough is very similar to traditional methods. For example the cross-section of a piece of shortcrust pastry should always be smooth and homogeneous, while a rich sponge mixture should cling to the spoon, and a sponge cake should turn out light and airy in texture no matter what type of flour is used.
Only the amount of liquid may vary depending on the degree of refinement of the ground flour.
Always check the temperature of your oven with a baking thermometer before cooking. Also, unless otherwise indicated, ingredients should be used at room temperature and should be fully prepared before you start baking.
So, now just get started and let your friends praise your cooking, while you enjoy healthier food that has been easy to prepare! Think how nice it will be to spoil your family with food that is so tasty and good for them. Happy baking.

Some Useful Facts About Grains

When you consider that the whole grain contains all the substances needed to produce a new plant it makes you realize how important the whole grain is for a healthy diet. It is, therefore, ironic that society is proud of having produced a refined white flour, an all-purpose flour, from which has been removed the husk of the grain and the oil containing germ, both high in food value. Through a study of modern ailments it has been found that in producing this refined flour the most nutritious substances have been discarded.

Wheat

Among the ancient Greeks wheat was the most widely used grain for making bread. So important was it to them that they considered it as one of their main gifts from "Mother Earth."
Today, wheat is still the most widely used grain for modern bread making. Its great usefulness in baking comes from the fact that 80% of its protein consists of gluten. This makes the dough rise well and gives it a firm, spongy texture. Whether you buy wheat flour ready ground or whether you grind your own grains, it has to be used immediately as it will not keep. Storing reduces the spicy aroma and nutritive substances, and it quickly becomes rancid.

Rye

Rye is about the same in nutrition as wheat, (rye is slightly higher in fiber), but it has a low gluten content. This means that the flour will not bind well and yeast alone is not sufficient to make dough rise. A sourdough has to be added to rye dough, which both enhances the distinctive rye flavor and gives a good crust to the baking.

Oats

At one time oats formed the staple diet (as groats or paps), which was later replaced by bread and potatoes. Oats, however, are a very nutritive grain as can be seen from their use in convalescent foods, containing plenty of protein, unsaturated fatty acids, vitamins B and E, zinc, manganese and silicic acid. But, as with rye, baking is difficult because the protein in oats prevents the flour from binding well. To counter this, other flours or eggs have to be added.
When buying oats make sure you obtain the beardless variety, from which the husks have not been removed. Husked out grains have little nutritional value. It is better to buy only whole grain oats, so make sure the grains are la-

Useful Facts About Grain

belled "with germ" or "real whole grain oats." Oats have a very high fat content and have to be ground in special mills, as they will clog the rollers or millstones of ordinary mills. If other types of grain are also used in the recipe, then the oats can be mixed with these and ground in the usual way.

Barley

Barley is said to be the oldest grain product in the world. Its high nutritive value made it the staple diet of the Egyptians, Babylonians and Romans, although it was not a popular food and was given mainly to slaves and livestock. Although barley is widely used in the production of beer and whiskey, it has yet to secure its place in the kitchens and bakeries of the world. This is probably due to the fact that the "beard" is extremely diffi-

spike, or particle millet and is as versatile in cooking as rice. It swells considerably during cooking and can be used in sweet or spicy dishes. It gives baking a crisp texture. Millet contains more minerals than other types of grain: manganese, phosphorous, iron and silicic acid. These are important in producing strong hair, nails and fibrous tissue.

Maize

After rice and wheat, maize is grain in the world. The grain grows in cobs, which are yellow when harvested, and contain many minerals and vitamins A, B and E. It is rich in protein and unsaturated fatty acids. However, as it is lacking in gluten, it has to be mixed with other flours or grist before baking. The best baking results are obtained with a mixture containing 30% maize flour. Maize grains are very hard

and today at least half the world's population could not exist without it. The three main types of rice grown are: round-grain, which becomes soft and glutinous with boiling; short-grain, used for making risottos; long-grain, which remains as firm grains even after boiling.

White rice is not used in health food diets because the polishing of the rice removes all the nutritive ingredients. Brown rice has had the coarse outer husk removed, but the germ and layers of silver skin enclosing the grain have been left intact. These contain protein, fat, minerals, vitamins, trace elements and fiber. They are particularly rich in vitamins E, B1, niacin, potassium, calcium, iron, sodium, cobalt, manganese, zinc and flourine. Brown rice, also known as unpolished rice, keeps its color

only allows it to be stored longer, but ensures that it retains 80% of its nutritive ingredients. Brown rice is available as par-boiled rice, which has a cooking time of only twenty minutes and can be stored for over a year.

Buckwheat

In spite of its name buckwheat is not a member of the wheat family. It derives its name from the composition of its grain-like triangular seeds and its usefulness in cooking. In fact it is a type of knot-grass which grows in poor, sandy soils. The seeds have a distinctive, slightly bitter flavor which blends in well with either sweet or spicy pastry. For making dough it is advisable to mix buckwheat flour with a high gluten content flour, e.g. wheatflour.

Buckwheat has a high nutritional value containing protein, unsaturated fatty acids, vitamin B, potassium, calcium, phosphorous, manganese, iron and silicic acid.

Types of Flour

Wholewheat Flour (or wholemeal flour)
—consists of the whole wheat (100%)
—good for bread-making, strong flavor

Wheat Meal Flour
—consists of 85% of the whole wheat
—more refined than wholemeal flour
—suitable for cakes and confectionery
—not as strong a flavor as wholemeal flour

Rye Flour
—gluten content is low and has to be mixed with high gluten wheat flour
—produces heavy dough, e.g. rye bread, pumpernickel

Stoneground Flour
—coarser than roller milled flour, it absorbs up to twice as much water
—high fiber content and short storage time

Malted Grain
—added malted grains give a distinctive flavor

The above illustration shows the flour kernel at the center of the grain, containing 75% starch and 10% protein; the germ at one side of the kernel, containing protein, nutritious oils and vitamins B and E; the aleurone layer, enclosing the flour kernel, containing fat, vitamins, minerals and some bran; the husk, a firm outer layer, containing minerals, trace elements, and fibers.

cult to remove. However, a newly cultivated beardless type is now available, and as it is rich in minerals and vitamins B and E, its use should become more popular. When mixed with wheat it bakes well to produce a good pastry.

Millet

Millet will grow in the poorest of soils and so is available in most countries. It grows as

and it is probably easier to buy them ready-ground. Maize is also available, already ground, as polenta, semolina, groats and grist, but like all whole grain products, because of its high fat content it can only be stored for a short period of time.

Rice

Rice has been cultivated for about the last 5,000 years,

when boiled and has a stronger flavor than white rice. However, it takes twice as long to cook and tends to break up when boiled. Like all whole wheat products brown rice can only be stored for a short time, and the expiry date should always be shown on the packet.

Par-boiled rice has undergone a special treatment which not

Alternative Sweeteners

Alternatives to sugar can be safely used to sweeten food, drinks and pastries ensuring a healthy diet. Ideally the best way is to get out of the habit of sweetening food, and scientific investigations have shown that giving sweetened food to babies increases their appetite for sugar throughout childhood and in some cases stays with them for the rest of their lives. Therefore, we should make every effort to substitute our sugar intake by natural or organic sweeteners.

Dried Fruits (unsulphurated): These are particularly useful for baking as they provide sugar, and other nutritive substances, such as trace elements, in a concentrated form. They contain a high percentage of natural fibers, stimulate the digestion and the whole metabolism. Unfortunately, they can also help to bring about malnutrition—just as all sugar containing sweeteners can.

Honey: This is a completely natural and pure sweetener. Bees are so sensitive to pesticides that minute amounts are enough to kill them. This means that impure or poisoned honey cannot exist. Also honey breaks up carbohydrates and stimulates the metabolism. In addition it contains a substance, found in human saliva, which hinders the growth of certain bacteria and improves the circulation. Honey also supplies energy very quickly as it takes less than 10 minutes to be absorbed into the bloodstream. Unfortunately, in baking, it loses a lot of its nutritive constituents, enzymes, acids, fructose, glucose and its distinctive aroma. When eaten in small quantities, however, it is still better than using refined sugar. Unless you want to give your baking a specific flavor it is not always necessary to use the best honey. Any wild honey is suitable. Naturally, this only applies to real pure honey not to artificial or honey substitute.

Maple Syrup: Sap is collected from the maple tree, treated and its water content reduced by evaporation. The finished product is what we call maple syrup. It contains 65% sugar and so only relative small amounts are needed for sweetening. A considerable amount of its vitamin content is lost when it is made into syrup but many other highly nutritive ingredients remain.

Beet (Golden) Syrup: This has very good baking qualities. When the cleaned and shredded sugar beets are stewed, the saccharose is broken up into fructose and glucose, and the gelatinizing plant fibers leave the cell membrane and mix into the beet syrup. After draining off the excess water, 78% of the syrup remains. Golden Beet syrup is widely used like jam, but it also gives a sweet strong flavor and rich brown color to both sweet and spicy baking.

Apple Syrup and Pear Syrup: These are obtained in the same way was as beet syrup and have the same baking properties while adding a richer fruitier flavor. But they have the drawback of being made from fresh apples and pears which often need reasonable proportions of additional white sugar. However, sugar-free syrups are available in shops but are usually about twice the price of ordinary syrup as double the volume of fresh fruit is required to make them.

Sufficient amounts of raw material are available to make more sugar-free syrups, if the demand becomes high enough. This means that customers would have to be prepared to pay a higher price initially to increase the demand and so bring down the price eventually.

Confectioners' Sugar: You may be surprised to find confectioners' sugar included in some of the recipes. This is purely for decorative purposes.

Delicious Everyday Baking

You do not have to wait for a special occasion to enjoy eating cakes. In this section the names of many of the recipes will be familiar to you but try them, you will realize the subtle differences in taste compared with traditional recipes. "Old German Cheesecake" made with freshly ground wheat and millet grains has a spicier and more piquant flavor than you would have believed possible. And the "Linzer Tart," sweetened with honey, dried apricots and maple syrup has a delicious fruity fragrance. The same can be said of the whole grain Kugelhupf and other rich sponge cakes. The same goes for cream puffs made from wheat and buckwheat and the numerous pastries made from yeast dough.

You will be surprised how delicious and rich cakes made of carrots, potatoes, stale bread, dried white beans and oats can be made to taste.

Spicy Rings

Makes 20 pieces

250 calories per serving
Preparation time: about 30 minutes
Baking time: about 50 minutes

¾ cup mixed dried fruit	
½ cup raisins	
3 tbs. rum	
1¼ cups butter	
Pinch salt	
1¼ cups honey	
5 eggs	
1 cup sour cream	
1 tsp. cinnamon powder	
1¾ cups wheat flour	
½ cup millet flour	
2 tsp. baking powder	
⅔ cup finely chopped almonds	
Butter to grease	
Graham crackers crumbs to line baking pan	

Rinse the dried fruit and raisins under hot water and dry well. • Chop finely and place in a bowl. Add the rum. Cover and leave to soak. • Pre-heat oven to 350°F. • Beat together the butter, salt and honey until very creamy. Add the eggs one by one. Stir in the cinnamon and sour cream. • Mix together the wheat flour, millet and baking powder and stir this into the mixture. Add the dried fruit and rum. • Grease an 11 in. diameter ring mold, or use two 7 in. diameter molds, line the mold with wholemeal crumbs. • Spoon the mixture into the mold and place on the lower shelf of the oven. • Bake a large mold for about 50 minutes (small ones 30 minutes). Test with a needle. • Leave in the mold to cool slightly, then remove to a wire rack.

Spiced Walnut Ring Cake

Makes 20 pieces

265 calories per serving
Preparation time: 30 minutes
Rising time: about 15 minutes
Baking time: about 1 hour

1¼ cups butter	
Pinch salt	
2 cups honey	
6 eggs, separated	
1 tsp. cinnamon powder	
½ tsp. cloves	
Pinch freshly grated nutmeg	
Pinch ground ginger	
2½ cups wheat flour	
½ cup millet flour	
½ cup linseed meal	
½ cup whole grain oats	
½ cup milk	
2 tsp. baking powder	
3 tbs. rum	
¾ cup finely chopped walnuts	
Butter to grease	
Graham cracker crumbs to line baking pan	

Beat together the butter, salt and honey until creamy. Add the eggs one by one and then spices. • Put to one side 3 tablespoons of wheat flour. • Mix together the remaining wheat, millet, linseed and oats. Spread this over the butter mixture. • Add the milk slowly and mix the ingredients to a smooth dough. Leave to stand for about 15 minutes. • Preheat oven to 350°F. • Mix together the baking powder and the 3 tablespoons wheat flour. Add this and the rum to the dough. Beat the egg whites until stiff and fold into the dough with the walnuts. • Grease an 11 in. diameter ring mold, or two 5 in. diameter molds, and line with graham cracker crumbs. • Spoon dough into the mold and bake on lower shelf of oven: large mold takes 1 hour, small molds 30 minutes.

Hazelnut Cake

Makes 15 pieces

290 calories per serving
Preparation time: about 35 minutes
Baking time: about 50 minutes

2 cups hazelnuts
⅔ cup butter
Pinch salt
½ tsp. cinnamon powder
1¼ cups honey
6 eggs
2 tbs. almond extract
Grated rind of 1 orange
1¾ cups wheat flour
½ cup buckwheat flour
2 tsp. baking powder
Butter to grease
Graham cracker crumbs to line baking pan

R oast hazelnuts in a large, dry pan, turning them continually until the skins burst open. Wrap them in kitchen towel and remove the skins by rubbing them off. Allow to cool and grind finely. • Beat together the butter, salt, cinnamon and honey until creamy. Add the eggs one by one, then the almond extract and grated orange rind. • Preheat oven to 350°F. • Mix together the wheat flour, buckwheat and baking powder. Add this to the butter mixture with the ground hazelnuts. • Grease 12 in. rectangular baking pan. Line with graham cracker crumbs. Spoon the mixture into the pan, smooth the surface. • Bake for about 50 minutes on a lower shelf of the oven. If it starts to brown too quickly cover with aluminum foil. • Test with a needle. When needle comes out dry remove the cake from the oven. Leave to cool in the pan for a few minutes before putting onto a wire rack.

Tip: To make it easier to remove the cake, line the pan with wax paper which is easy to peel off when completely cool.

Carrot Cake

Makes 16 pieces

305 calories per serving
Preparation time: about 1½ hours
Baking time: 50-60 minutes

¾ cup carrots
6 eggs, separated
4 tbs. water
1¾ honey
3 tbs. kirsch
2 pinches ground cloves and cinnamon powder
Pinch salt
½ cup wheat flour
½ cup buckwheat flour
1 tsp. baking powder

1¾ cups freshly ground hazel nuts
1 cup freshly ground walnuts
Butter to grease
Graham cracker crumbs to line baking pan
1-2 oranges
1½ cups cream
2 tbs. maple syrup
¼ cup finely chopped pistachio nuts

Peel the carrots, rinse and dry. Grate finely. • Beat together egg yolks, water, honey and kirsch until light and fluffy. Add the cinnamon and cloves. • Preheat oven to 350°F. • Beat the egg whites until stiff. • Mix together the wheat flour, buckwheat flour, baking powder, hazelnuts and walnuts. Blend in carefully with the egg yolk mixture. Cover with the egg white and carefully fold in the carrot. •

Grease the base of a spring-release pan. Do not grease the sides as this stops the dough from rising evenly. Line with graham cracker crumbs. • Spoon the mixture into the mold and bake on a low shelf for 50-60 minutes. • Test with a needle. When needle comes out dry remove the cake from the oven. Leave to cool in the pan for a few minutes before removing to a wire rack. • Just before serving wash the oranges, dry them and grate into long, thin strips. • Beat the cream until stiff and sweeten with maple syrup. Cover the cake completely with cream and sprinkle with orange strips and pistachios. Serve immediately.

Tip: The cake can be baked one to two days before it is eaten to give a richer, fuller flavor. • The cake can also be frozen without losing its flavor, but should not be covered with cream until just before serving. • If you want to decorate it with cream stars put 4 tablespoons of the whipped cream into a piping bag with a star-shaped nozzle to pipe onto the 16 individual slices. • You can substitute almonds for the hazelnuts or walnuts, which will produce a tangier flavor. Freshly roasted hazelnuts can also be used to give the cake a stronger, nuttier taste.

Linzer Tart

Makes 16 pieces

250 calories per serving
Preparation time: about 45 minutes
Cooling time: about 45 minutes
Baking time: about 50 minutes

¾ cup butter

Pinch salt

1 cup honey

2 egg yolks

2 pinches cinnamon powder

Grated rind of ½ lemon

1¼ cups finely ground almonds

1¾ cups wheat flour

⅔ cup dried apricots

2 tbs. raspberries fresh or unsweetened

3 tbs. maple syrup

3 tbs. raspberry liqueur (optional) (or extract)

Butter to grease

Graham cracker crumbs to line baking pan

Wheat flour for rolling out dough

1 egg yolk

Beat together the butter, salt, honey, egg yolks, cinnamon and lemon rind until creamy. • Mix the wheat flour and almonds and add a quarter of this to the butter mixture. Knead in the rest of the wheatflour mixture to form a ball of dough. Wrap in foil and cool in a refrigerator for 45 minutes. • Meanwhile, wash apricots under hot water, dry and rinse. • Wash fresh raspberries in cold water, dry and purée. Thoroughly de-frost frozen fruit if this is used. • Sieve the purée and mix with the apricots and maple syrup. Bring to a boil in a saucepan and simmer, stirring continuously, until it thickens. Add the raspberry liqueur, if used, and

set aside to cool. • Preheat oven to 350°F. • Grease a spring-release quiche pan and line with graham cracker crumbs. Then line with three-quarters of the dough to give a 1 in. high edge. Prick several times with a fork and cover with the purée. • Roll out remaining dough on a lightly floured surface and cut into strips. Place these on the purée to form a lattice design. Press the ends of the strips firmly into the edge and brush with whisked egg yolk. • Bake in the center of the oven for about 50 minutes. Allow to cool slightly before removing from pan to a wire rack.

Tip: For a tastier tart add a pinch of ground cloves or a little ground ginger. • Finely ground hazelnuts, walnuts or pistachio nuts can be substituted for almonds.

Variations:

Linzer Tart with Fig Marzipan
Prepare the dough as before. While it is cooling in the refrigerator the marzipan can be prepared. • Wash 1 cup dried figs in hot water. Dry and remove stalks. Chop the fruit finely. • Blanch 1 cup almonds in boiling water for 2 minutes. Immerse in cold water and remove skins. Dry and purée in a liquidizer. • Mix together into a smooth paste the almond purée, chopped figs, ½ cup honey, 2 tablespoons cognac or rum and almond liqueur. • Prepare the quiche pan and dough base as before and cover with the fig marzipan mixture. Place strips of dough to form a lattice design, brush with whisked egg yolk and then bake as above.

Black and White Cake

Makes 15 pieces

260 calories per serving
Preparation time: about 50 minutes
Baking time: about 50 minutes

| ⅔ cup butter |
| 2 cups honey |
| 5 eggs |
| Pinch salt |
| 3 tbs. cream |
| 2¼ cups wheat flour |
| ½ cup maize flour |
| 1 tsp. baking powder |
| ½ cup finely ground almonds |
| Pulp from 1 vanilla pod |
| 2 tbs. cocoa |
| 2 tsp. instant coffee powder |
| 2 pinchs allspice |
| 3 tbs. rum |
| Butter to grease |
| Graham cracker crumbs to line baking pan |

Beat together butter, honey, eggs, salt and cream until creamy. • Mix together wheat-flour, maize and baking powder. Blend the flour smoothly into the butter mixture, divide the mixture in half. • To one half add vanilla and almonds, to the other add coffee powder, cocoa, all-spice and rum. • Preheat oven to 350°F. • Line a rectangular baking pan with wax paper. Grease with butter and line with graham cracker crumbs. • Alternately spoon in the light and dark mixtures, to make an attractive pattern. • Place cake on low shelf of oven and bake for about 50 minutes. Test with needle: when needle comes out dry the cake can be taken out of the oven. • Leave to cool for a few minutes before turning out onto a wire

rack. Remove paper and turn cake over again.

Orange Almond Cake

Makes 15 pieces

330 calories per serving
Preparation time: about 50 minutes
Baking time: 50-60 minutes

| ½ cup butter |
| 2¼ cups honey |
| 6 eggs |
| Pinch salt |
| Grated rind of 1 orange |
| 2 tbs. plain yogurt |
| ½ cup millet flour |
| ½ cup buckwheat flour |
| 1½ cups wheat flour |
| 2 tsp. baking powder |
| 1¾ cups freshly ground almonds |
| Butter to grease |
| Graham cracker crumbs to line baking pan |
| Juice of 2 oranges |
| 1 liqueur glass orange liqueur |
| 1 tbs. rum |

Beat together the butter, 1¼ cups honey, eggs, salt, or-ange rind and yogurt until creamy. • Mix together the millet, buckwheat, wheat flour, baking powder and almonds. Blend this into the butter mixture. • Preheat oven to 350°F. • Line a rec-tangular baking pan with wax paper. Grease it with butter and line with graham cracker crumbs. Spoon in the mixture and smooth face. • Bake on a low shelf for 50-60 minutes. Test with needle: when needle comes out dry remove cake from oven. • Allow to cool for a few minutes before turning out onto a wire

rack. Remove wax paper and turn cake over again. • Heat up the orange juice with the remaining honey, orange liqueur and rum, stirring continuously. Leave to cool for a few minutes. • Prick all over the top of the cake and slowly pour the orange mixture over the cake until all the liquid is absorbed. Leave to cool completely.

Old German Cheesecake

Makes 16 pieces

280 calories per serving
Preparation time: about 45 minutes
Cooling time: about 30 minutes
Baking time: about 1 hour

1¾ cups wheat flour
½ cup millet flour
Pinch salt
Grated rind of ½ lemon
1 egg yolk
1 whole egg
2 tbs. honey
½ cup hard butter
Butter to grease
Graham cracker crumbs to line baking pan
For the filling:
⅔ cup raisins
4-5 tbs. rum
3¼ cups ricotta cheese
½ cups cream
5 eggs, separated
⅔ cup honey
Juice and rind of ½ lemon
Pulp from 1 vanilla pod
Pinch salt
⅓ cup finely chopped almonds
¼ cup linseed meal

To make the base: mix together the wheat flour, millet, salt and lemon rind. Make a well in the middle of the mixture. • Whisk the egg yolk and the whole egg and add the honey. Pour this into the well. • Place small pieces of butter around the edge of the flour. Thoroughly chop the mixture until crumbly, then knead to a smooth dough. Shape into a ball, wrap in foil and cool in refrigerator for 30 minutes. • Grease an 11 in. round baking pan and line with graham cracker crumbs. • To make the filling: wash the raisins in hot water, dry, and leave to soak in the rum in a covered bowl. • Beat together the cheese, cream, egg yolks, honey and lemon juice until creamy and add the lemon rind and vanilla. • Preheat oven to 400°F. • Line the baking pan with the dough, pressing it down firmly. Prick the dough with a fork. • Whisk the egg whites until stiff, add salt and place on top of the cheese mixture. Add the almonds, linseed meal, raisins and rum and thoroughly mix all the ingredients together. • Spoon this filling into the baking pan. Smooth the surface and bake on the lower shelf of the oven for about 1 hour. If the surface browns too quickly cover it with foil. • When cooked, remove from the oven and leave to cook for a short while before putting on a wire rack. Leave overnight before cutting.

Tip: The baking time will vary slightly depending on how moist the cheese is. Always test with a needle and if the cake is not fully cooked just bake for a little longer at a lower temperature (310°-330°F) so that the surface does not brown too fast.

Raspberry Cream Puffs

Makes 20 pieces

140 calories per serving
Preparation time: about 1 hour
Baking time: 25-30 minutes

For the dough:
1 cup water
½ tsp. salt
⅓ cup butter
1 cup wheat flour
½ cup buckwheat flour
4-5 eggs
Butter to grease
For the filling:
1⅓ cups fresh raspberries, or unsweetened frozen
2 cups heavy or whipping cream
3-4 tsp. honey
3 tbs. raspberry liqueur

Add the salt and butter to the water and bring to a boil. • Mix together wheat flour and buckwheat flour and add to a boiling liquid. Stir continuously with a wooden spoon until the mixture thickens to a doughy consistency. Place dough in a bowl and mix in 1 egg. Leave dough to cool until lukewarm. • Mix in the remaining eggs one by one. Make sure that each egg is thoroughly mixed in before adding the next. Before adding the final egg you should make the "dough test": it should be elastic and stiff enough not to fall from the spoon. If the mixture seems a little too stiff whisk the final egg and add only as much of it as is needed. • Preheat oven to 400°-425°F. • Grease one or two flat baking trays and make walnut sized mounds of the mixture, using a piping bag with a star-shaped nozzle or using two spoons. • Space these widely on the baking trays and bake for 25-30 minutes until golden brown on middle shelf. Do not open the oven during the first 15 minutes or the dough will collapse. • After baking, immediately cut each puff in two with a sharp knife and leave to cool. • Wash fresh raspberries in cold water, dry and hull. With frozen fruit defrost and dry. • Beat cream until stiff. Mix with honey and raspberry liqueur. Spoon into a piping bag with a star-shaped nozzle. Pipe cream onto lower half of puff, press in raspberries and cover with top half. Serve immediately.

Tip: If you wish to decorate the cream puffs pipe cream dots on the top and sprinkle with cocoa powder. • An alternative decoration is to sprinkle the tops with confectioners' sugar. This small amount of sugar could not affect a diet. • The cream puffs are just as delicious with different fruits or fillings such as honey ice cream. • The puffs can be deep frozen without the fillings.

Crullers

Makes 20 pieces

115 calories per serving
Preparation time: about 1½ hours

½ cup water
½ tsp. salt
½ cup butter
½ cup wheat flour
½ cup buckwheat flour
½ cup fine maize groats
3-4 eggs
½ tsp. cinnamon powder
¼ cup rum butter for deep frying

Oil to grease

2 tbs. honey

2 tbs. maple syrup

3 tsp. lemon juice

2 tsp. rum

Add the salt and butter to the water and bring to the boil. Put to one side. • Mix together wheat flour, buckwheat flour and maize. Add this to the liquid. Return the pan to the cooker and stir the mixture continuously with a wooden spoon until it thickens to a doughy consistency. • Put the dough in a bowl and mix in 1 egg. Leave to cool until lukewarm. Add the remaining eggs one by one. Before adding the last egg make the dough test (as described for raspberry cream puffs) and add as much of the last egg as is needed. Add the cinnamon. • Heat the rum butter to 330°F in a deep fryer. Cut 5 in. squares of wax paper and coat with oil. • Spoon the dough into a piping bag with a star-shaped nozzle and pipe circles onto the wax paper. • Gently immerse 3 crullers in the hot fat and cook until golden brown. Make sure the crullers do not touch each other as they will stick together. • When cooked, remove from the fat and place on wax paper for a couple of minutes before transferring to a serving dish. • To make the glaze, melt the remaining butter and add the maple syrup, honey, lemon juice and rum. Bring to a boil, stirring continuously until it thickens and, while still hot, spoon onto the crullers.

Vanilla Cream Almond Yeast Cake

Makes 20 pieces

305 calories per serving
Preparation time: about 1½ hours
Standing, rising and cooling time: 3-4 hours
Baking time: about 25 minutes

3½ cups wheat flour
½ cup linseed flour
¼ cup fresh yeast
1 cup milk
1¾ cups honey
1 egg
Pinch salt
½ tsp. vanilla extract
Grated rind of ½ lemon
1¼ cups soft butter
Butter to grease
1¼ cups flaked almonds
½ cup sunflower seeds
½ cup cream
For the filling:
1½ cups water
Pinch salt
1 cup millet flour
½ cup milk
1 cup honey
½ tsp. vanilla extract
1 egg yolk
⅔ cup soft butter
3 tbs. rum

Mix wheat flour and linseed flour together in a bowl and make a well in the center. Crumble yeast into the well, mix with a little milk, some of the flour and work into a smooth dough. • Cover and put to one side in a warm, draft-free place. After 15 minutes it should have swelled and formed bubbles. • Add the remaining milk, ½ cup honey, the egg, salt, vanilla and lemon rind. Place small pieces of butter around the edge of the mixture. Knead well and beat until the dough leaves the sides of the bowl and still shows bubbles. • Cover and leave to stand for at least 30 minutes. • Meanwhile grease a baking tray with butter and preheat oven to 425°F. • Knead dough once more and roll out on a greased baking sheet. Place this in a warm spot and leave for a further 15 minutes. • Melt the remaining butter in a saucepan, add the rest of the honey, almonds, sunflower seeds and cream and bring to a boil. Allow to cool slightly before spreading smoothly over the dough. • Place on middle shelf of oven and bake for about 25 minutes until golden brown. Remove from oven to a wire rack. • To make the filling, boil water and salt, stir in the millet, stir continuously, boil for 5 minutes. Add milk, reboil and leave to stand for 45 minutes. • Beat a little of the millet paste with the honey, vanilla, egg yolk and rum and add to the remainder of the paste. Whisk egg whites until stiff, fold them into the mixture. Place the bowl in a saucepan of cold water and stir mixture occasionally until cool. • Beat butter until creamy and gradually mix into the millet paste mixture. Cool in the refrigerator for a few minutes. • Cut cake base in half horizontally and spread the bottom half with the filling. Cut the almond covered top half into 20 equal sized pieces. Place these on top of the cream filling and cut through the base between the slices to make 20 small cakes.

Pastry Cheesecake

Makes 20 pieces

330 calories per serving
Preparation time: about 30 minutes
Rising time: about 45 minutes
Baking time: 35-40 minutes

3½ cups wheat flour

1 cup millet flour

¼ cup fresh yeast

1 cup lukewarm milk

1¾ cups honey

¾ cup butter

Pinch salt

Butter to grease

2¼ cups cream cheese

1¼ cream

3 eggs, separated

Grated rind of 1 lemon

1 tsp. vanilla extract

1 cup raisins

1 cup freshly chopped almonds

½ cup flaked almonds

Mix together the wheat flour and the millet, make a well in the center and crumble the yeast into it. Mix with a little milk and some of the flour to a dough. • Cover and leave to stand for 15 minutes. • Mix in the remaining milk, ½ cup honey, ¼ cup butter and salt and knead into a smooth dough, beat until the mixture leaves the side of the bowl and begins to bubble. Leave to stand for a further 30 minutes. • Preheat oven to 400°F. • Grease a baking pan with butter. Knead dough a little more, roll out and place in baking pan. • Beat together cream cheese, remaining honey, cream and egg yolks until creamy and add lemon rind and vanilla. • Beat egg whites until stiff. • Wash and dry raisins and add to the cream cheese mixture. Add the

ground almonds and egg whites. • Cover the dough with the mixture and sprinkle on the flaked almonds. Dot with remaining pieces of butter and bake in the middle of the oven for 35-40 minutes.

Sesame and Nut Crumb Cake

Makes 20 pieces

320 calories per serving
Preparation time: about 35 minutes
Rising time: about 1 hour
Baking time: 25-30 minutes

3½ cups wheat flour

½ cup linseed flour

¼ cup fresh yeast

1 cup lukewarm milk

½ cup honey

1 egg

Pinch salt

½ tsp. cinnamon powder

¼ cup soft butter

Butter to grease

For the crumbs:

¾ cup butter

1¼ cups honey

1 egg yolk

1 tsp. cinnamon powder

2¼ wheat flour

½ cup sesame seeds

½ cup chopped hazelnuts

3 tbs. cream

Mix together wheat flour and linseed flour, make a well in the center and crumble the yeast into it. Mix with a little milk and some of the flour to a dough. • Cover and leave to stand for 15 minutes. • Add honey, the remaining milk, the egg, salt, cinnamon and butter cut into small pieces. • Work into

a smooth dough and beat until the mixture leaves the sides of the bowl and begins to bubble. Leave to stand for 30 minutes. • Preheat oven to 440°F. • Grease baking sheet with butter. Knead dough and roll out onto the sheet. Leave in a warm place for a further 15 minutes. • To make the crumbs, beat together the butter, honey, egg yolk and cinnamon until creamy. Stir in half the flour. Mix the remaining flour with sesame seeds and nuts to make coarse crumbs. • Spread the dough with cream and cover with the crumbs. Bake in the middle of the oven for 25-30 minutes.

Date and Pine Nut Braid

Makes 20 pieces

290 calories per serving

Preparation time: about 50 minutes
Rising time: about 1 hour
Baking time: about 35 minutes

| 3½ cups wheat flour |
| 1 cup buckwheat flour |
| ½ cup millet flour |
| ¼ cup fresh yeast |
| 1 cup lukewarm milk |
| 2 eggs |
| 1 cup honey |
| Pinch salt |
| 2 pinches cinnamon powder |
| 2 pinches freshly ground cardamon |
| Grated rind and juice of ½ orange |
| ⅔ cup soft butter |
| 2 cups dried dates |
| 2 liqueur glasses white rum |
| 2 tbs. orange liqueur |
| ½ cup pine nuts |
| 2 egg whites |

| 3 egg yolks |
| ½ cup pistachio nuts |
| Wheat flour for rolling out dough |
| Melted butter for greasing and brushing |
| 2 tbs. cream |

Mix together wheat flour, buckwheat flour and millet. Make a well in the center, crumble the yeast into it and mix with a little milk and some of the flour to make a dough. • Cover and leave to stand in a warm draft-free spot for 15 minutes or until it begins to bubble. • Add remaining milk, eggs, ½ cup honey, salt, cinnamon, cardamon and rind and juice of orange. Put small pieces of butter around the edge of the mixture and knead into a smooth dough. Knead until mixture leaves the sides of the bowl and starts to bubble. • Cover and leave to stand for 30

minutes. • Stone dates, chop finely and place in a small bowl. Add rum and orange liqueur. Cover and leave to soak. • Chop pine nuts and fry in a dry frying pan, stirring continuously until golden yellow. • Melt butter and allow to cool until lukewarm. • Whisk egg whites until stiff and add the remaining honey. Fold in dates and linseed. Add 2 beaten egg yolks, half the pistachio nuts and the melted butter. • Knead the dough again on a floured surface and divide into three. Roll out each piece to a 8 × 20 in. rectangle, brush with melted butter and spread evenly with the filling. • Roll up lengthwise and seal edges well. Braid the dough rolls, firmly press down the ends and place on a greased baking sheet. Leave to stand in a warm place. • Preheat oven to 400°F. • Beat together the remaining egg yolk and cream and

brush the braid with it. Bake on a low shelf for about 35 minutes until golden brown. • Chop the remaining pistachio nuts. Remove braid from oven, brush with a little melted butter and cover with the nuts. Leave to cool before slicing.

Tip: Instead of using dates, the braid can be made with figs, apricots or plums.

Apple and Marzipan Rose Cake

Makes 16 pieces

320 calories per serving
Preparation time: about 45 minutes

Rising time: about 1 hour 20 minutes

Baking time: about 40 minutes

3½ cups wheat flour

1 cup millet flour

¼ cup fresh yeast

1 cup lukewarm milk

1¼ cups honey

Pinch salt

¼ cup soft butter

2 cups hazelnuts

3 tbs. Calvados or rum

½ cup raisins

4 baking apples

Juice ½ lemon

Wheat flour to roll out dough

Butter to grease

Graham cracker crumbs to line pan

1 egg yolk

2 tbs. cream

Flaked almonds to sprinkle on cake

Confectioners' sugar to dust cake (optional)

Mix together wheat flour and millet flour, make a well in the center and crumble yeast into it. Add a little milk and mix with some of the flour to a dough. • Cover and leave to stand in a warm draft-free place for 20 minutes or until it starts to bubble. • Add ½ cup honey, salt, remaining milk and butter in small pieces and knead to a smooth dough. Beat until mixture leaves the side of the bowl and starts to bubble. • Cover and leave to stand until it has doubled in size. • Grind 2 cups hazelnuts finely, add remaining honey and Calvados or rum. Blend into a smooth marzipan. • Chop the remaining hazelnuts, wash and dry the raisins and peel, core and grate apples. Add lemon juice to apples. • Knead the dough into a ball and roll out on a floured surface to a 12 × 24 in. rectangle. Spread the marzipan evenly over it. Sprinkle with raisins, apples and nuts. •

Roll up the dough lengthwise and cut into 2 in. long pieces with a sharp knife. Grease an 11 in. round baking pan with butter and line with graham cracker crumbs. • Place filled dough pieces in pan so that they are not touching each other. Leave to stand until they have expanded enough to stick together. • Preheat oven to 400°F. • Whisk together egg yolk and cream. Brush over the cake and sprinkle with flaked almonds. Bake on a low shelf for about 40 minutes. Leave to cool slightly before removing from baking pan and placing on a wire rack. Dust with confectioners' sugar if desired.

Tip: This cake can be prepared in various ways. Pears, thinly cut pineapples, peaches and apricots can be used instead of apples. • The hazelnuts can be substituted with almonds to make almond

marzipan. The cake can also be sprinkled with flaked almonds.

Potato Cake

Makes 16 pieces

220 calories per serving
Preparation time: about 45 minutes
Cooling time: 12-24 hours
Baking time: about 50 minutes

1⅓ cups potatoes
Pinch of salt
½ cup raisins
3 tbs. rum
¼ cup dried bananas
6 eggs, separated
1 cup honey
Juice and grated rind of 1 orange
1 cup freshly ground almonds
½ cup buckwheat flour
1 tsp. baking powder

Butter to grease
Graham cracker crumbs or chopped almonds to line baking pan
6 oz. milk chocolate

Scrub potatoes in cold water and cook whole in salted water until par-boiled. Immerse in cold water, peel and leave to cool thoroughly, if possible overnight. • Grate the potatoes finely. Wash and dry raisins, place in bowl with rum. Cover and leave to soak. • Chop bananas finely. • Beat together egg yolk, honey, orange juice and rind until creamy. • Preheat oven to 350°F. • Mix together almonds, buckwheat flour and baking powder. Spread this over the egg yolk mixture and place potatoes on top. Beat the egg whites stiffly with a pinch of salt and spoon over the potatoes, mixing all these ingredients together. Add raisins, rum and chopped banana. • Grease an 8 in. diameter round baking pan with butter and line with graham cracker crumbs or chopped almonds. • Spoon mixture into pan, smooth the surface and bake on low shelf for about 50 minutes. Test with a needle. The needle should come out dry. • The baking time can vary depending on the type of potatoes you use. After baking leave the cake to cool slightly before placing it on a wire rack. • Crumble the honey chocolate into a small basin. Place in a saucepan of hot water and stir continuously until the chocolate has melted. Remove the basin from the pan and continue stirring until the chocolate begins to thicken. • Pour the chocolate over the cake, smooth evenly with a long broad knife, and let it run down the sides. Al-low this glaze to harden completely before cutting.

Tip: As an additional decoration, sprinkle the cake surface with chopped almonds or decorate with small, homemade marzipan balls. • Prepare the marzipan according to recipe substituting almonds for hazelnuts. Finally, place one larger ball of marzipan in the center of the cake.

Wine and Pear Cake

Makes 16 pieces

145 calories per serving
Drying time: about 30 minutes
Preparation time: about 1 hour
Baking time: 40-45 minutes

| ¼ cup stale pumpernickel |
| ⅔ cup stale whole grain bread |
| ½ cup dried pears |
| 1 glass red wine |
| 6 eggs, separated |
| 1 cup pear syrup |
| 2 tbs. pear liqueur (optional) |
| Juice and rind of ½ orange |
| ½ tsp. cinnamon powder |
| Pinch ground cloves |
| Pinch salt |
| ½ cup freshly ground walnuts |
| 1 cup coarsely ground wheat flour |
| Butter to grease |

Graham cracker crumbs to line baking pan
Confectioners' sugar to dust cake (optional)

Preheat oven to 200°F. • Crumble the pumpernickel and sprinkle it on a dry baking pan. Cook on middle shelf of the oven for about 30 minutes depending on how moist the bread is. Remove and leave to dry and cool completely. • Meanwhile, crumble the whole grain bread into a bowl. • Wash pears under hot water, dry and chop finely. Mix this with the wine into the crumbled bread and leave, covered, to soak. • Grind the pumpernickel finely. Beat together egg yolks, pear syrup, pear liqueur, juice and rind of orange until creamy; add cinnamon and cloves to taste. • Beat the egg whites and salt until stiff and place on the egg yolk mixture. •

Preheat oven to 350°F. • Mix together walnuts, pumpernickel crumbs, wheat and the pear mixture, thoroughly blending all the ingredients. • Grease a circular baking pan and line with graham cracker crumbs. Spoon in the dough and smooth the surface. Bake on a low shelf for about 45 minutes. • Test with a needle. Leave to cool for a few minutes before turning out onto a wire rack. • Dust with a little confectioners' sugar.

Tip: As confectioners' sugar is only used for decoration, it is often easy to design your own pattern. This is done by cutting out a paper stencil (or using a paper doily) in any attractive shape and dusting the confectioners' sugar over it. Less confectioners' sugar is used in this way.

Raspberry Cream Roll

Makes 12 pieces

285 calories per serving
Preparation time: about 45 minutes
Baking time: 10-12 minutes
Cooling time: 50-60 minutes

For the sponge:
5 eggs, separated
Pinch salt
3 tbs. warm water
1¼ cups honey
Grated rind of ½ orange
1½ cups wheat flour
1 tbs. baking powder
For the filling and decoration:
1¼ tbs. white gelatin
½ tbs. red gelatin (if available or total of 2 tbsp. unflavored gelatin)
1⅓ cup raspberries

2 eggs, separated
1 tbs. warm water
1 cup honey
Grated rind of ½ orange
Juice of 1 orange
2 cups plain yogurt
Pinch salt
1½ cups cream

Line a baking sheet with wax paper and leave the paper overlapping at one end. • Preheat oven to 400°F. • Beat together the egg yolks, salt, water, honey and orange rind to a creamy mixture. • Whisk the egg whites until stiff and place them on the egg yolk mixture. • Mix the wheat and baking powder and shake this over the egg white. Mix these ingredients together. • Spread this dough evenly on the baking pan and bake in the middle of the oven for 10-12 minutes until golden yellow. • Dampen a clean tea towel with hot water, wring out and cover the cake with it. Carefully turn over the baking sheet and remove the wax paper. Roll up the sponge using the tea towel and leave to cool. • Dissolve the gelatin. • Wash and dry the raspberries, hull them and select 12 to keep for decoration. • Purée the remaining fruits and sieve. • Stir the egg yolks with water, honey, orange rind and juice. Add the yogurt, beating until creamy, then add the fruit purée. Thicken with the dissolved gelatin. • Put 3 tablespoons of the cream filling into a piping bag with a star-shaped nozzle and cool in refrigerator. • As soon as the raspberry cream starts to thicken fold in the remaining cream. Carefully roll out the sponge and cover with the raspberry cream. Roll up again, still using a tea towel, and decorate the top with 12 cream rosettes and raspberries.

Variations: Chocolate Roll with Peach Cream and Pistachios • Melt 2 oz. honey chocolate in a basin placed in a saucepan of hot water. Remove and leave to cool. • Prepare the sponge mixture as above using vanilla extract instead of orange rind. Add cold, but liquid chocolate to the prepared dough just before baking. • Bake and cool as above, but for the filling use 1⅓ cups of finely chopped peaches (either fresh or canned, unsweetened). Mix these with ¼ cup of chopped pistachios and cream. • Fill the roll and decorate as above.

Fruit Teacake

Makes 20 pieces

190 calories per serving
Preparation time: about 45
minutes
Baking time: about 1½ hours

1⅓ cups raisins
⅔ cup stoned plums
1 cup dried apricots
¼ cup dried apples
2 tbs. rum
2 tbs. orange liqueur
⅔ cup almonds
1 cup hazelnuts
4 eggs
Pinch salt
½ cup honey
Grated rind of ½ orange
1 cup instant whole grain oatflakes
1 tsp. baking powder
Butter to grease

Graham cracker crumbs to line
baking pan

Wash the dried fruits in hot water, dry and chop. Mix with orange liqueur and rum, cover, leave to soak. • Meanwhile, chop the almonds and hazelnuts. • Preheat oven to 350°F. • Beat together the eggs, salt, honey and grated orange rind until creamy. • Mix together the oatflakes and baking powder and add this to the mixture. Also add the dried fruit, rum, hazelnuts and almonds. • Grease a 12 in. long rectangular baking pan with butter and line with oatflakes. Spoon in the dough and smooth the surface. • Bake on the low shelf of the oven for about 1½ hours. Test with a needle. Leave to cool for a few minutes before placing onto a wire rack. Leave overnight for the flavor to develop fully.

Fruit Cake

Makes 20 pieces

235 calories per serving
Preparation time: about 45
minutes
Baking time: about 1 hour 10
minutes

⅔ cup raisins
¼ cup candied lemon peel
¼ cup candied orange peel
4 tbs. rum
⅔ cup almonds
¾ soft butter
Rind of 1 lemon
1½ cups wheat flour
1 cup buckwheat flour
½ maize flour
3 tsp. baking powder
Butter to grease
Graham cracker crumbs to line baking pan
4 egg whites

Pinch salt
Confectioners' sugar to dust cake
(optional)

Wash raisins in hot water and dry. Dice orange and lemon candied peels, mix with the raisins then cover with the rum and leave to soak. • Meanwhile, scald the almonds with boiling water and remove the skins. Dry and chop. • Beat together the butter, egg yolks, honey and lemon rind until creamy. • Mix together the three flours with the baking powder and stir into the mixture. • Grease a 12 in. long rectangular baking pan with butter and line it with graham cracker crumbs. • Preheat oven to 350°F. • Beat the egg whites and salt until stiff then add to the mixture. Also add the rum, raisins and almonds. • Mix all the ingredients thoroughly and spoon them into

a baking pan. Smooth the surface and bake on the low shelf of the oven for about 1 hour 10 minutes. Test with a needle. • Leave to cool for a few minutes and then place on a wire rack. If desired dust with icing sugar.

Pecan Nut and Apple Pie

Makes 16 pieces

370 calories per serving
Preparation time: about 1 hour
Cooling time: 3-4 hours
Baking time: about 1 hour

For the dough:
2¼ cups wheat flour
½ cup buckwheat flour
Pinch salt
⅔ cup firm butter
1 tsp. vanilla extract
1 egg yolk
1 egg

2 tbs. honey
3 tbs. ice cold water
Wheat flour to roll out dough
For the filling and decoration:
¼ cup raisins
2 tbs. candied orange peel
1⅓ cup baking apples
Juice of ½ lemon
¼ cup butter
1 cup honey
¼ pecan nuts, shelled and peeled
1¾ cups cream
2 tbs. rum or brandy

Mix the wheat flour, buckwheat flour and salt together on a work surface. Cut the cold butter into small pieces, add it to the flour and chop until the mixture becomes crumbly. • Make a well in the center and fill with vanilla extract, egg yolk, honey and the egg. Knead into a smooth dough, adding the water as necessary. Wrap in foil and cool in a refrigerator for at least 3-4 hours, or overnight. • Cover the work surface with foil, dust with flour and roll out the dough on it. • Place the bottom of an 11 in. diameter spring release pan on the dough and cut out the pie top. Cut a small whole in its center. Keep a small amount of dough for decoration. • Line the pan with the rest of the dough forming a 1½–2 in. edge. Prick the base with a fork. • Preheat oven to 400°F. • For the filling, wash the raisins in hot water and dry. • Chop the candied orange peel finely. • Wash the apples, quarter them, core and grate them roughly. Add the lemon juice. Mix this with the raisins and candied peel. • Slowly melt the butter and add the honey. Chop the pecan nuts and add them to the honey. Stir in the cream and bring to a boil. Remove the saucepan from the cooker, add raisins, apples, orange peel and rum or brandy. • Spoon the filling into the baking pan. Cover with the pie top, using the foil to lift it. Remove the foil and firmly press down the top around the edge. • Shape some decorative leaves out of the remaining dough and place on the top. • Whisk egg yolk and brush the surface of the pie with it. • Bake in the middle of the oven for about 1 hour. Cool for a few minutes, then place it on a wire rack.

Tip: Walnuts can be used for this pie instead of pecan nuts.

Austrian Oatflake Cake

Makes 12 pieces

460 calories per serving
Preparation time: about 30 minutes
Baking time: about 1 hour
Cooling time: 12-24 hours

⅔ cup raisins

3 tbs. rum or brandy

½ cup butter

2 eggs, separated

1¼ cups honey

1¾ cups soft, whole grain oatflakes

1 cup milk

Grated rind of ½ lemon

1½ sachets baking powder

Pinch salt

Butter to grease

Graham cracker crumbs to line baking pan

2 cups cream

Redcurrants to decorate

1¾ cups redcurrants, unsweetened and stewed

3 tbs. rough, whole grain oatflakes

¼ cup finely chopped pistachio nuts

Wash the raisins in hot water and dry them well. Place in a small bowl with the rum or brandy, cover and leave to soak. • Meanwhile cream together the butter, honey and egg yolks. • Mix together the two types of oatflakes and add these to the mixture. Add the milk. Beat this mixture until creamy. • Preheat oven to 350°F. • Add to the mixture the grated lemon rind, raisins, rum or brandy and baking powder. • Beat the egg whites and salt until stiff. Fold this into the mixture. • Grease an 11 in. diameter spring-release pan and line it with graham cracker crumbs. Spoon the mixture into the pan, smooth the surface and bake on a lower shelf for about 1 hour. • Test with a needle. Cool for a few minutes before placing on a wire rack and leaving to cool overnight. • Just before serving cut the cake in half horizontally. • Beat the cream until stiff. Put a third of it into a piping bag with a star-shaped nozzle and leave to cool in the refrigerator. • Wash the redcurrants, dry and remove the stalks. • Divide the rest of the cream into two and add the stewed redcurrants to one half. Cover the base of the cake with this mixture. Then place the other half of the cake on top. Cover the cake completely with the remainder of the cream. • Sprinkle the edge and center with oatflakes. Deco-rate each of the 12 slices with cream rosette, sprinkle with pistachio and decorate with the redcurrants.

Tip: When preparing the dough make sure that the baking powder mixes well with the other ingredients to insure that the cake will rise evenly. It is best to sieve it over the dough. Alternatively it can be combined with 1-2 teaspoons of wheat flour. • A few soft oatflakes can also be mixed together with the baking powder before working them into the dough.

Bon Herculour Ring Cake

Makes 12 pieces

555 Calories per serving
Preparation time: about 1½ hours
Baking time: about 1 hour
Cooling time: about 1 hour

For the dough:

1 cup butter
2 cups honey
5 eggs, separated
Pinch salt
Grated rind of 1 lemon
2 tbs. rum
1¾ cups wheat flour
½ cup oatmeal flour
1 tsp. baking powder
Butter to grease
Graham cracker crumbs to line baking pan

For filling and decoration:

1 cup water
½ cup millet flour
½ cup milk
1 cup honey
½ tsp. vanilla extract
1 egg, separated
Pinch salt
1 cup butter
⅔ cup finely chopped almonds
3 tbs. rough ground oatmeal flakes
Oil for brushing
3 tbs. rum
12 almonds

To make the dough mix together the butter, honey, egg yolks, salt, rum and grated lemon rind to a smooth cream. • Preheat oven to 350°F. • Mix together the wheat flour, ground oats and baking powder. Sieve over the dough mixture. • Beat egg whites until stiff and fold them into the mixture. • Grease a ring mold with butter and line it with the graham cracker crumbs. Fill it with the mixture and bake for about 1 hour on a lower shelf of the oven. • Test with a needle. Leave to cool for a few minutes then put it on a wire rack. • To make the butter cream, boil the water, add the millet flour and stir continuously with a whisk. Continue to boil and stir, mixing in the milk. Leave, over a very low heat, to cook for 45 minutes. • Put to one side 1 tablespoon of honey. • Whisk the rest of the honey with the vanilla, egg yolk, and a little of the cooked millet. Stir well into the rest of the millet mixture. Leave this on a low heat but do not allow it to boil. • Beat the egg whites and salt until stiff and fold them into the millet mixture. Remove from the heat, cover and leave to stand for about 15 minutes. Place the saucepan in cold water and allow to cool. • Heat together 2 tablespoons butter, the remaining honey, chopped almonds and the oatflakes. Mix thoroughly to a golden caramel. • Grease a piece of foil with oil and spread the caramel over it. Leave this to cool. Put this into a plastic bag and crush with a rolling pin. • Cream the remaining butter and gradually add the cold millet mixture. Add rum to taste and cool in the refrigerator until firm, but not hard. • Cut the cake twice horizontally. Put 3 tablespoons of the buttercream into a forcing bag with a star-shape nozzle. • Divide the remaining buttercream into 3. Spread one-third on the bottom layer of the cake. Place middle layer on top of this and spread this and another one-third of the cream. Finally place on top layer of cake and spread remaining cream over the top and edge. • Sprinkle the top and sides of the cake with the crushed caramel. • Pipe a cream rosette onto each of the 12 slices and then place an almond on each.

Marzipan Teacake

Makes 20 pieces

315 calories per serving
Preparation time: about 1 hour
Baking time: about 55 minutes
Cooling time: about 12 hours

1⅓ cups peeled almonds
1¼ cups honey
1 cup soft butter
5 eggs
Pinch salt
½ tsp. vanilla extract
5 tbs. orange liqueur
Rind and juice of 1 orange
1¾ cups wheat flour
1 cup buckwheat flour
1 tsp. baking powder
½ cup almonds finely ground
Butter to grease
Graham cracker crumbs to line pan
1¼ cups unsweetened marmalade
602 grams milk chocolate

Grind the almonds finely and mix them thoroughly with 1 cup to make the marzipan. Cover, and put to one side about 1¼ cups of this mixture. • Beat together the butter, eggs, remaining honey, and the remaining marzipan until creamy. Add salt, vanilla, 2 tablespoons orange liqueur and the rind and juice of half the orange. • Preheat oven to 350°F. • Mix together the flours, baking powder and the creamy mixture into a dough. • Grease a 12 in. long deep rectangular baking pan, line it with the graham cracker crumbs and spoon in the dough. • Bake for about 55 minutes on a lower shelf. Test with a needle. Leave

to cool on a wire rack. • Cut the cake three times horizontally. • Mix the remaining orange juice with the rest of the orange liqueur and sprinkle this over each layer of cake. • Spread half the marmalade onto the bottom layer of cake. Cover with the second layer and spread the remaining marzipan on this. Place the third layer on this and cover with the remaining marmalade and finally add the fourth layer of cake. • Put the chocolate into a basin in a saucepan of hot water and stir until liquid. Allow chocolate to cool a little and spread over the cake.

Poppy Seed and Almond Cake

Makes 12 pieces

495 calories per serving
Preparation time: about 30 minutes

Baking time: about 1 hour 25 minutes

1 cup butter
8 eggs, separated
2 cups honey
2 glasses cognac or grappa
1 vanilla pod
1 tsp. cinnamon powder
Pinch ground mace
2¼ cups seedless grapes
Pinch salt
1¼ cups freshly ground almonds
1¾ cups freshly ground poppy seeds
½ cup wheat flour
1 tsp. baking powder
Butter to grease
Graham cracker crumbs to line pan
1-2 tsp. confectioners' sugar for decoration (optional)

Cream the butter. Mix in the egg yolks, honey and cognac or grappa. • Slit open the vanilla pod and scrape out the pulp. Add this and the ground mace to the mixture. Beat it until it is very creamy. • Wash the raisins in cold water, dry them and remove the stalks. • Preheat oven to 350°F. • Beat the egg whites and salt until they are stiff. Fold half of these egg whites into the mixture. Place the remaining egg white on top. • Mix together the ground almonds, poppy seeds, wheat flour and baking powder and mix this thoroughly into the rest of the mixture. • Grease an 11 in. diameter round spring release pan and line it with the graham cracker crumbs. • Spoon in ¾ of the mixture and smooth the surface. Sprinkle with the raisins and cover with the remaining mixture. • Bake on a lower shelf of the oven for about 45 minutes then reduce the oven temperature to 300°F and bake for about a further 30-35 minutes. • If the surface starts to brown too quickly cover it with foil. • At the end of the baking time test the cake with a needle: if the needle still has some of the mixture sticking to it then continue baking for a short time. Switch off the oven and leave the cake in it for 5-10 minutes. • Remove the cake from the oven, cover with a towel and leave it for 10-15 minutes before removing from the pan. Leave to cool on a wire rack. If desired the cake can be dusted with confectioners' sugar.

Tip: It is better to use seedless grapes as the relatively long baking time might cause the seeds to taste slightly bitter. • If you can only buy grapes with seeds remove them with a small skewer.

• Instead of grapes other fruit, such as pitted cherries or pear slices, can be used.

Macaroon and Rhubarb Cake

Makes 16 pieces

220 calories per serving
Preparation time: about 30 minutes
Baking time: about 35 minutes

½ cup butter
1¾ cups honey
2 eggs
Pinch salt
½ tsp. cinnamon powder
Grated rind of ½ lemon
1 cup wheat flour
½ cup buckwheat flour
1 tsp. baking powder
Butter to grease
½ cup graham cracker crumbs
½ cup finely chopped hazelnuts
2¼ cups rhubarb
3 egg whites
1 cup coarsely chopped hazelnuts

Cream together the butter, eggs and half the honey. Add salt, cinnamon powder and the grated lemon rind and mix thoroughly until creamy. • Mix together the wheat flour, buckwheat flour and baking powder. Sieve over the mixture and stir in thoroughly. • Preheat oven to 350°F. • Grease an 11 in. diameter spring release pan with butter and line it with some of the graham cracker crumbs. • Mix the remaining crumbs with the finely chopped hazelnuts. Spoon the mixture into the baking pan, smooth the surface and cover with the crumbs and hazelnuts. • Wash the rhubarb in cold water and dry it. Then trim it and cut it into ½-1 in. long pieces. Place on the hazelnut layer. • Beat the egg whites until stiff, then beat in the remaining honey until the mixture is firm. Spread this over the cake and bake in the middle of the oven for about 35 minutes until slightly brown. • The baking time can vary depending on the moisture content of the rhubarb. It is therefore better to test the cake with a needle. If the cake needs further baking cover the surface with foil to prevent it burning. • After baking leave the cake in the pan to cool for a few minutes before placing it on a wire rack.

Tip: The graham cracker and nut layer separating the cake from the rhubarb prevents any moisture from the fruit spoiling the cake base. It also gives the cake a delicious, spicy, nutty flavor. • Oatflakes can be used instead of the graham cracker crumbs. These should be slightly roasted in a dry frying pan. • Walnuts, almonds or coconut flakes can be used instead of the hazelnuts. • Various unsweetened berries may be used instead of the rhubarb.

Old Viennese Chocolate Cake

Makes 16 pieces

510 calories per serving
Preparation time: about 1 hour
Baking time: 50-60 minutes
Cooling time: 12-24 hours

1 cup almonds
14 oz. milk chocolate
1 cup soft butter
1½ cups honey
8 eggs, separated
1½ cups wheat flour
½ cup buckwheat flour
¼ cup millet flour
½ tsp. baking powder
Pinch salt
Butter to grease
1 jar (1 lb.) unsweetened apricot jam
1 cup cream
½ tsp. vanilla extract

Cocoa powder for dusting (optional)

Scald the almonds in boiling water then place in cold water. Remove the skins by rubbing them. Dry well and grind finely. • Chop 7 oz. of the chocolate, place it in a basin and put this in a saucepan of hot water. Stir the chocolate until it has melted. • Cream the butter and mix in the egg yolks and 1¼ cups of the honey until very creamy. Then fold in the melted chocolate. • Mix together the wheat flour, buckwheat flour and baking powder. Sieve over the mixture. • Preheat oven to 350°F. • Beat the egg whites and salt until stiff and add to the mixture. Then add 1 cup of the ground almonds and thoroughly mix together all these ingredients. • Grease an 11 in. diameter spring-release pan with butter and line it with the remainder of the almonds. Spoon in the mixture and bake on a lower shelf for 50-60 minutes. • Test with a needle. Allow to cool before placing on a wire rack. Leave to cool completely, overnight if possible. • Put the apricot jam in a basin and place this in a saucepan containing hot water. Put on a low heat, do not allow the water to boil, and stir until the jam is runny. Allow it to cool slightly. • Cut the cake in half horizontally. Spread a third of the jam over one half and cover with the top layer of cake. Spread the remaining jam over the surface and edge of the cake and leave to dry slightly. • Cut the rest of the chocolate into wide flakes. Chop finely one third of these flakes. • Beat together the cream, remaining honey and the vanilla until stiff. Put 2 tablespoons of the cream into a forcing bag with a star-shaped nozzle. Spread the rest of the cream over the cake. • Sprinkle the edge with the chopped chocolate. Decorate the top of the cake by piping cream around the edge. Then cover the center with the chocolate flakes and dust with cocoa powder if desired.

American Cheesecake

Makes 12 pieces

315 calories per serving
Preparation time: about 35 minutes
Baking time: about 1 hour

¾ cup granola biscuits with fruit sugar
1 cup maple syrup
¼ cup soft butter
Butter to grease

| 2¾ cups cottage cheese |
| 1¼ cups cream |
| 5 eggs, separated |
| Grated rind and juice of ½ lemon |
| ½ tsp. vanilla extract |
| Pinch salt |

Put the granola biscuits in a plastic bag and crumble with a rolling pin. • Mix together ¼ cup of the maple syrup, butter cut into small pieces and the crumbs. Knead into a smooth dough. • Grease a 10 in. diameter spring-release pan and spoon in the crumb mixture and smooth over the base. • Preheat oven to 350°F. • Whisk together the cottage cheese, cream, egg yolks and vanilla extract. Add the rest of the maple syrup, lemon juice and grated lemon rind and mix in thoroughly. • Beat the egg whites and salt until stiff and fold

into the mixture. Spoon this into the baking pan and bake in the middle of the oven for about 1 hour. • If the surface starts to brown too quickly, cover with foil. Allow the cake to cool for a few minutes before placing on a wire rack.

Tip: A few raisins could be added to the cheese mixture to give a fruity flavor.

Honey Nut Tart

Makes 16 pieces

550 calories per serving
Preparation time: about 45 minutes
Cooling time: about 30 minutes
Baking time: 50-60 minutes

| For the dough: |
| 2¼ cups wheat flour |
| 1 cup buckwheat flour |
| ½ cup maize flour |
| Pinch salt |
| ½ cup freshly ground almonds |
| 2 pinches vanilla extract |
| 1 egg |
| 1 egg yolk |
| 3 tbs. kirsch |
| 1¼ cups cold butter |
| Butter to grease |
| Graham cracker crumbs to line pan |
| Wheat flour to roll out dough |

| For the filling and decoration: |
| 1¾ cups coarsely ground hazelnuts |
| 1¾ cups coarsely ground walnuts |
| 2 tbs. butter |
| 1¼ cups honey |
| 1¾ cups cream |
| ½ tsp. cinnamon powder |
| Pinch salt |
| 3 tbs. kirsch |
| 1 cup finely chopped honey chocolate |
| 2 egg yolks |
| 1 egg |

To make the dough, knead all the dough ingredients together to form a ball and leave to cool for 30 minutes. • Grease an 11 in. diameter spring-release pan and line with graham cracker crumbs. • Slightly roast the hazelnuts in a frying pan and allow to cool. • Melt the butter and honey in a saucepan and remove from the heat before stirring in the cream, cinnamon, salt and kirsch. Add the nuts, chocolate and egg yolks. • Preheat oven to 400°F. • Line the baking pan with about three quarters of the dough, forming a 1 in. high edge. Spoon in the filling. Roll out the rest of the dough on the floured work surface to make the top. Place on top of the filling. •

With a sharp knife cut a lattice pattern on the top of the tart. Brush with beaten egg. • Bake in the middle of the oven for 50-60 minutes and allow to cool on a wire rack.

Apricot and Almond Rice Flan

Makes 12 pieces

445 calories per serving
Preparation time: about 1 hour
Cooling time: about 1 hour
Baking time: about 1 hour 10 minutes

1½ cups wheat flour
1 cup millet flour
½ cup freshly ground almonds
Salt
1 egg
1¼ cups honey
¾ cup cold butter
1½ cups milk
1 cup natural short grain rice
Grated rind of ½ lemon
2¼ fresh apricots
3 eggs, separated
1 liqueur glass apricot pit liqueur (Amaretto di Saronno Originale).
1¾ cups coarsely chopped almonds
Wheat flour for rolling out dough
Butter to grease
Graham cracker crumbs to line pan
Pulses for baking blind

Mix together wheat flour, millet flour, salt and ground almonds on a working surface and make a well in the center. • Fill the well with the egg and 1¼ cups honey and place the butter, cut into small pieces, over the flour. • Knead all the ingredients to a smooth dough, wrap in foil and cool in the refrigerator for about 1 hour. • Bring the milk and salt to a boil, add the rice and lemon rind and re-boil, stirring continuously. Reduce to a very low heat and leave the rice to cook for about 30 minutes. Remove it from the heat, put into a bowl and place this in a saucepan of cold water, stirring occasionally, until it is cool. • Meanwhile, wash the apricots in cold water and pit them. (Skin them if desired). • Cream the rest of the butter and mix in the egg yolks, one by one, and the remaining honey. Stir in the chopped almonds, apricot liqueur and rice. Cover and place to one side. • Roll out the dough on a floured working surface. • Preheat oven to 400°F. • Grease an 11 in. diameter spring-release pan with butter and line it with graham cracker crumbs. Then line with the dough, forming a 1½–2 in. high edge. Prick the base several times. Cover the dough with wax paper and fill with dried pulses. Bake on a lower shelf of the oven for about 20 minutes. • Meanwhile, beat the egg whites until stiff and add this to the rice mixture. • Remove the pastry from the oven and take out the pulses and paper. Spoon half the rice mixture into the pastry and cover with the apricot halves, cut-side uppermost. Then cover with the remaining rice mixture. • Bake on the lower shelf again for 50 minutes. Allow to cool a little before placing on a wire rack.

Tip: Using the dried pulses when baking blind stops the pastry edge from collapsing. The pulses can be used again if they are left to cool completely before being stored in a dry place.

Banana and Pineapple Chelsea Buns

Makes 20 pieces

205 calories per serving
Preparation time: about 45 minutes
Rising time: about 1 hour
Baking time: 15-20 minutes

| 2½ cups wheat flour |
| ½ cup millet flour |
| 1 cup buckwheat flour |
| ¼ cup fresh yeast |
| 1 cup lukewarm milk |
| 1 egg yolk |
| ½ cup honey |
| Pinch salt |
| ⅓ cup soft butter |
| ⅓ cup raisins |
| ¾ cup dried bananas |
| 4 tbs. white rum |
| 1 small pineapple, about 1¾ lbs |
| Butter to grease |
| Wheat flour for rolling out dough |
| ½ cup flaked coconut |
| 1 egg |
| 2 tbs. cream |

Mix together the wheat flour, millet flour and buckwheat flour. Make a well in the center and crumble the yeast into it. Add a little milk and some of the flour and mix to a dough. Cover this and leave it to stand in a warm draft-free-place for 15 minutes until the dough has risen and is beginning to bubble. • Add the remaining milk, honey, egg yolks and salt. Chop ¼ cup of butter into small pieces and work all the ingredients into a smooth dough. Beat the dough until it leaves the sides of the bowl and begins to bubble. Cover and leave to stand for about 30 minutes until the vol- ume has doubled. • Meanwhile, wash the raisins in hot water and dry. • Dice the dried bananas finely. Mix this with the white rum and raisins and leave to soak, covered. • Trim and peel the pineapple and remove the hard core. Shred the fruit pulp finely. • Grease a baking tray with butter. Knead the dough again and roll it out to a 12 x 16 in. rectangle, on a floured work-ing surface. Melt the remaining butter and brush this over the dough. • Mix together the raisins, rum, bananas, pineapple and co-conut flakes and spread them over the dough. • Roll up the dough from the longer side. Cut into 1 in. thick slices with a sharp knife. Place them on the baking tray, leaving enough space be-tween each piece so they will not stick together when cooking, and leave to stand for about 15 min-utes. • Preheat oven to 400°F. •

Whisk together the egg and cream. Brush the pastry with this and bake in the middle of the oven for 15-20 minutes. • Cool on a wire rack and serve fresh.

Tip: When preparing a yeast dough, all the ingredients used should be at room temperature. Milk, butter and eggs should be taken out of the refrigerator well before they are needed and the flour should be warmed if it has been stored in a cold place. • These buns can be frozen as soon as they come out of the oven. They should be wrapped immediately, separately in foil, and labelled and dated. Then when they are wanted they only have to be heated up again for a few minutes in a hot oven.

Baking for Special Occasions

You can enjoy deliciously rich cakes and still keep to a healthy diet if you use whole grain flours in your baking.

This section shows you how to make such special cakes: Peach and Flake Surprise Cake, with rye and wheatmeal flour, Blueberry Cream Cake made with buckwheat, Chestnut Cream Cake with fresh cherries, "Furst-Puckler" Buttercream Cake and Strawberry Cream Sponge Cake.

For a special treat there is the Honey Ice Cream cake which can be prepared well before a party. And for a very special occasion the three-tiered wedding cake, made of rice and decorated with home-made marzipan and wine cream, traditionally brings good luck to all young couples.

The classic Christmas cakes have not been forgotten, e.g. the fruit cake and the butter fruit loaf, which is given extra flavor by the addition of exotic fruits.

Pineapple and Cream Cake

Makes 16 pieces

320 calories per serving
Preparation time: about 1 hour
Baking time: about 30 minutes

For the dough
5 large eggs
1¾ cups honey
5 tbs. hot water
1¾ cups wheat flour
½ tsp. baking powder
½ cup walnuts, finely chopped
2 tbs. butter
Butter to grease
Graham cracker crumbs to line baking pan
For filling and decoration:
1 small pineapple (about 1¾ lbs.)
2 liqueur glasses rum
2 cups cream
2 tbs. maple syrup
½ cup finely chopped walnuts
16 walnuts -for final decoration

Beat together the eggs, honey and hot water, with an electric mixer, for about 15 minutes until it is foamy and syrupy. • Preheat oven to 350°F. • Whisk the wheat flour, baking powder and walnuts into the mixture. Melt the butter and add it while still hot. • Grease a 10 in. diameter spring-release pan with butter and line with graham cracker crumbs. Spoon in the mixture and bake on a lower shelf of the oven for about 30 minutes. • Test with a needle. Allow to cool for a few minutes before placing on a wire rack. Leave to cool overnight. • Peel and core the pineapple. Cut about a quarter of the fruit into pieces for decoration. Chop the rest of the fruit. • Cut the cake in half horizontally and sprinkle both halves with rum. Beat the cream until stiff and add the maple syrup. Mix about three-quarters of it with the pineapple and the walnut mixture. • Spread the mixture over one half of the cake and place the other half on top. • Keep 3 tablespoons of the remaining cream for decoration and spread the rest over the top of the cake. • Decorate each of the 16 slices with a dot of cream, pineapple pieces and walnut halves. • Serve immediately.

Tip: Chocolate and carob can also be used to make the gateau: Mix 1-2 teaspoon of carob with the baking powder before mixing into the dough, and sprinkle the edge of the finished gateau with flaked honey chocolate. • To make a richer cake, melt ½ cup of honey together with the butter and add this to the mixture. Also add a little more baking powder to the flour, so that the cake will rise evenly. • Different fruits can also be used: fresh raspberries, peaches, tropical fruits and unsweetened frozen fruits. Any fruit used should be dried well so that it does not spoil the cream.

Nut-Cream Fig Slices

Makes 10 pieces

450 calories per serving
Preparation time: about 45 minutes
Baking time: 10-15 minutes

¼ cup dried figs
1 cup finely ground hazelnuts
Butter to grease
6 eggs, separated
4 tbs. warm water

1¼ cups honey

Grated rind of ½ lemon

Pinch salt

1 cup wheat flour

3 cups cream

Pinch vanilla extract

2 fresh figs

2 tsp. finely chopped pistachio nuts

Rinse the figs in hot water, dry and chop finely. Mix with the hazelnuts. • Line a baking sheet with grease proof paper and grease it with butter. • Preheat oven to 400°F. • Cream together the egg yolks, water, 1 cup of honey and the lemon rind. • Beat the egg whites and salt until stiff and then fold them into the mixture. • Add the wheat flour, figs and hazelnuts to the mixture and stir in thoroughly. • Spread this over the wax paper and bake in the middle of the oven for 10-15 minutes. • After baking turn out onto a baking board covered with foil. Remove the wax paper and allow to cool. • Meanwhile, beat together the cream, remainder of the honey and the vanilla until stiff. Spoon about a quarter of this into a piping bag with a star-shaped nozzle. • Wash, peel and slice the figs. Cut the cake in half lengthways and cover one layer with half the cream. • Cut the other layer in half lengthways again and then cut it across 4 times to make 10 separate pieces. Place these on top of the cream and cut completely through the cake to make 10 slices. • Decorate each piece with the remaining cream, figs and pistachio nuts.

Wine, Cream and Raspberry Cake

Makes 12 pieces

295 calories per serving
Preparation time: about 1 hour
Baking time: about 25 minutes
Total cooking time: about 2 hours 15 minutes

For the dough:

1¼ cups wheat flour

½ cup buckwheat flour

½ cup freshly ground peeled almonds

Pinch salt

Scraped out pulp ½ vanilla pod

½ cup sour cream

½ cup honey

⅓ cup butter

Butter to grease

Graham cracker crumbs to line baking dish

For garnish and decoration

1 tbs. white gelatin

1 egg

2 egg yolks

½ cup honey

1 tbs. lemon juice

½ cup dry white wine

1 cup cream

2 tbs. raspberry liqueur

2¼ cup raspberries

3 tbs. finely chopped pistachio nuts (optional)

To make the dough, mix together the wheat flour, buckwheat flour, almonds, salt and vanilla pulp on a work surface. Make a well in the center. • Whisk together the sour cream and honey and place it in the well. Cut the butter into small pieces and place on the flour. • Chop the dough until crumbly and then knead into a smooth dough. Wrap it in foil and cool in the refrigerator for about 1 hour.

• Preheat oven to 400°F. • Grease an 11 in. diameter fluted pie dish and line with graham cracker crumbs. Line with the dough, prick with a fork and bake in the middle of the oven for 20-25 minutes. • When cooked, cool the base on a wire rack for about 1 hour. • Meanwhile, dissolve the gelatin and leave to stand according to the instructions on the packet. • Whisk together the egg, egg yolks, honey, lemon juice and wine in a bowl. Place the bowl in a saucepan of hot water and beat the mixture until foamy and syrupy. Do not bring to a boil as eggs will curdle. • Remove the bowl from the saucepan, and dissolve the gelatin in the cream, stirring continuously. Then place the bowl in a pan of cold water and stir it occasionally as it cools. • Meanwhile, beat the cream until it is very stiff and then fold

half of it into the gelatin mixture together with the raspberry liqueur. • Spread this mixture evenly on the cake base and place it in the refrigerator until completely set. • Wash the raspberries under cold water and dry well. Hull them and place as many as possible onto the cream mixture. • Sweeten the rest of the cream with a little honey and pipe it onto the raspberries through a piping bag with a star-shaped nozzle. Make a lattice shaped pattern with the piped cream and sprinkle with chopped pistachio nuts. Serve immediately.

Tip: For a stronger fruit flavor, sieve about ¾ cup raspberries and purée them. Then add them to the wine cream before it sets. • Also you can use alternate sheets of red gelatin if you want to give the cake a more colorful appearance.

Raspberry and Kiwi Fruit Slices

Makes 10 pieces

360 calories per serving
Preparation time: about 45 minutes
Baking time: about 12 minutes
Cooling time: about 30 minutes

For the dough:
5 eggs, separated
1¾ cups honey
3 tbs. hot water
Pinch of salt
1 cup buckwheat flour
½ cup wheat flour
½ tsp. baking powder
For filling and decoration
1⅓ cup raspberries, fresh or unsweetened, frozen
2 tbs. honey
2 tbs. white rum
1 tbs. honey or vanilla liqueur
2 cups cream
4 kiwi fruits

Preheat oven to 400°F. • Beat the egg yolks in a bowl with the water and honey to make a very creamy mixture. • Mix together the wheat flour, buckwheat flour and baking powder. • Beat the egg whites until stiff and slide into the egg yolk cream. Sprinkle the blended flours onto this and thoroughly fold in all the dough ingredients. • Line a baking sheet with wax paper and double this along the open edge, if the sheet has one, to stop the dough from running while baking. Grease the paper with butter and spread the dough evenly onto it. • Place immediately on the middle shelf of the oven and bake for about 12 minutes until the sponge is a light yellow. Do not let the sponge go dry or hard. • Turn the sponge out im-mediately onto a foil covered work surface and remove the greaseproof paper; use a little water if needed. Leave the sponge to cool. • Meanwhile wash, dry and hull the fresh raspberries. Slightly thaw if frozen. • Mix the honey, rum and honey or vanilla liqueur together over a low heat, stirring continu-ously and not allowing to over-heat. Pour this mixture over the raspberries and set to one side, covered, for about 25 minutes. • Then drain the liquid off the fruit, using a sieve, and keep this to one side. Also select a few of the best raspberries and keep them for final decoration. • Now cut the base of the sponge in half lengthways. • Beat the cream until stiff and put three-quarters of it in the refrigerator. Gently mix the rest of the cream with the reserved fruit liquid. • Peel the kiwi fruits and cut them into small slices. Again keep a few of them to one side for final decoration. Fold the rest of them with the raspberries into the cream and spread this mixture over one half of the sponge. • Cut the other piece of sponge in half lengthways and across four times to make 10 pieces. Place these on top of the cream layer and cut completely through the cake to make 10 slices. • Cover and decorate the slices with the remaining cream, raspberries and kiwi fruits. Serve immediately.

<u>Tip</u>: Other combinations of fruit can be used for this cake; straw-berries and fresh pineapple, peaches and blackberries or ripe pears and blueberries. The blackberries and blueberries will color the cream but will not de-tract from the delicious flavor.

Blueberry Cream Cake

Makes 16 pieces

455 calories per serving
Preparation time: about 1 hour
Baking time: about 1 hour
Cooling and standing time:
overnight

| ¾ cup soft butter |
| 2 cups honey |
| 2 tbs. brandy |
| 6 eggs, separated |
| ½ tsp. vanilla extract |
| Pinch salt |
| 2¼ cups buckwheat flour |
| 2¼ cups freshly ground almonds |
| ½ tsp. baking powder |
| Butter to grease |
| Graham cracker crumbs to line baking pan |
| 1½ cups cream |
| 1½ cups blueberries (unsweetened) |
| ½ cup pistachio nuts, finely chopped |

Chop the butter into small pieces, in a bowl, and beat until foamy. Stir in about 1¾ cups of the honey, brandy and egg yolks. Beat to a creamy mixture. Add the vanilla. • Preheat oven to 350°F. • Beat the egg whites until stiff and add them to the mixture. • Mix together the buckwheat flour, almonds and baking powder. Sieve this over the mixture and stir all the ingredients together thoroughly. • Grease an 11 in. diameter spring-release pan with butter and line it with graham cracker crumbs. • Spoon in the mixture and immediately bake on a low shelf of the oven (if the mixture is allowed to stand for any length of time the egg whites will sepa- rate and the dough will not rise evenly). • Bake for about 1 hour, test with a needle and remove from the oven. Allow to cool slightly before placing on a wire rack and leave to stand over- night. • Just before serving cut the cake in half horizontally. • Beat the cream until stiff and add the rest of the honey. • Drain the blueberries in a sieve (keep the juice for future use). • Mix to- gether three-quarters of the blue- berries with one-third of the cream. Spread this over one half of the cake and cover with the other half. • Spoon one-third of the remaining cream into a pip- ing bag with a star-shaped nozzle and spread the rest of the cream over the top and edge of the cake. • Decorate each of the 16 slices with a cream rosette and the rest of the berries. • Sprinkle pistachio nuts along the edge and serve immediately.

Tip: To make a less rich cake with fewer calories replace the cream filling with blueberry jam and decorate the cake with con- fectioners' sugar and berries only. Also without the cream the cake can be kept for a few days.

Peach and Flake Surprise Cake

Makes 16 pieces

205 calories per serving
Preparation time: about 1½ hours
Total baking time: about 1 hour

½ cup water
Pinch salt
¼ cup butter
½ cup wheat flour
½ cup rye flour
3-4 eggs
1 tsp. carob powder
Butter to grease
Wheat flour to dust
2¼ cups ripe peaches
Juice ½ lemon
6 tbs. water
4 tbs. honey
2 tbs. peach or almond liqueur
3 tbs. flaked coconut
2 cups cream

Chop the butter into small pieces and mix with the salted water in a saucepan. Bring to a boil, remove the pan from the heat and add both the flours. • Return the saucepan to the heat and cook the mixture, stirring continuously until it forms a doughy consistency. • Place the dough in a bowl and stir in 1 egg. Allow it to cool until lukewarm and add the remaining eggs one by one. Thoroughly mix in each egg before adding the next one. Add the carob with the last egg. • Preheat oven to 425°F. • Grease a 10 in. diameter spring-release pan with butter and dust with flour. Line with one-third of the dough and bake in the middle of the oven for 20 minutes until lightly brown. • The dough will rise slightly and appear flaky. • Remove the pastry from the oven and leave to cool on a wire rack. Bake two more bases in the same way. • Put boiling water into a bowl and scale the peaches for 1-2 minutes. Dip them in cold water and remove the skins. Halve, pit and slice the fruit. • Put the lemon juice, water, honey and liqueur into a saucepan and bring to a boil. Add the peach slices and cook for a couple of minutes. Remove the saucepan from the heat and allow the fruit to soak for 2-3 minutes. • Remove the fruit and drain. Leave to cool. Re-boil the liquid and continue boiling until it thickens and is reduced in volume to about 2 tablespoons Leave to cool. • Fry the coconut flakes in a dry frying pan until pale yellow, remove to a place and allow to cool. • Beat the cream until stiff and add the cooled liquid. Place one-third of the cream in a piping bag with a star-shaped nozzle and put to one side together with 16 peach slices. • Mix together the rest of the fruit and cream. Spread half the mixture on one cake base, place another on top, cover with the remaining cream and place the third cake layer on top. • Decorate the top with 16 cream rosettes, to mark the 16 slices, and top each rosette with a peach slice. Sprinkle with coconut flakes and serve immediately.

Tip: Naturally, if you have an oven which heats to the same temperature throughout (fan-assisted) you can bake all three bases at the same time.

Hazelnut Cream Cake

Makes 16 pieces

365 calories per serving
Preparation time: about 1 hour
Baking time: about 45 minutes
Cooling time: about 3 hours

10 oz. milk chocolate
6 eggs, separated
4 tbs. warm water
1¼ cup honey
½ tsp. vanilla extract
2 cups freshly ground hazelnuts
¼ cup buckwheat flour
Salt
Butter to grease
2 cups cream
16 hazelnuts

Grate 4 oz. of the chocolate. Preheat oven to 350°F. • Beat together the egg yolks, water, honey and vanilla until very creamy. • Mix together the ground hazelnuts, buckwheat flour and grated chocolate. Add to the egg yolk mixture. • Beat the egg whites until stiff, and then to the mixture and stir all the ingredients thoroughly. • Grease the base of an 11 in diameter spring-release pan and spread one-third of the mixture into it. Bake in the middle of the oven for about 15 minutes. • Leave the rest of the mixture to stand in a cool place. • Remove the cake from the oven and allow to cool on a wire rack. • Bake two more sponges from the remaining mixture and allow them to cool. • Beat the cream until stiff and spoon 2-3 tablespoons into a piping bag with a star-shaped nozzle • Crumble the rest of the chocolate into a bowl and place in a saucepan of hot water. Stir until it has melted. • Dip the hazelnuts in the chocolate, with a fork, then place them on wax paper to allow the chocolate to harden. • Spread one layer of the cake with half the cream, cover with the second layer and the remaining cream and top with the third layer. •

Spread the chocolate over the top and edge of the cake and allow to harden. • Decorate each of the 16 slices with a cream rosette and a chocolate coated nut.

Chestnut and Cherry Cream Cake

Makes 16 pieces

515 calories per serving
Total preparation time: about 2 hours
Cooling time: about 1 hour
Setting time: 12-24 hours

| 7 cups chestnuts |
| 3 cups milk |
| Pinch salt |
| Grated rind of ½ lemon |
| 1 vanilla pod |
| 1¼ cups honey |
| ¾ tbs. gelatin |
| ½ cup butter |
| 4 tbs. kirsch |
| 1 jar (about 1½ lbs. fruit weight) unsweetened sour cherries |
| 3 cups cream |
| ½ cup flaked almonds |

Preheat oven to 400°F. • Prick the chestnuts a couple of times at the pointed end and roast on a dry baking sheet for about 15 minutes until the shells burst open. Take them out of the oven, remove the shells and skins. • Chop the chestnuts coarsely and add the milk, salt and lemon rind. Pour into a saucepan. • Bring to a boil, cover and simmer until the chestnuts are very soft. • Remove the vanilla pod and strain the mixture through a sieve or purée in a blender. • Melt the butter into this mixture, stirring well. Dissolve the gelatin completely in hot water and add to the mixture with the kirsch. Place in a refrigerator and leave to cool. • Drain the cherries and keep the juice for future use. • Beat 2 cups of the cream until stiff. As soon as the chestnut mixture starts to set mix in the cream. • Line an 11 in. diameter spring-release pan with wax paper. Spoon half the mixture into it. Put to one side 16 cherries and spread the rest evenly on top of the mixture. Cover with the rest of the mixture and cool in a refrigerator for 12-24 hours. • Just before serving, lightly roast the flaked almonds in a dry frying pan and allow them to cool. • Beat the rest of the cream until stiff. • Remove the cake from the baking pan and take off the wax paper. Spread some of the cream around the edge and sprinkle with the flaked almonds. • Put the remainder of the cream in a piping bag with a star-shaped nozzle. Decorate each of the 16 slices with a cream rosette and a cherry. • Serve immediately or leave in the refrigerator until required.

Tip: Keep the cherries that are to be used for decoration in cherry juice in the refrigerator overnight, so that they will not become dry and shrivelled. • Dry well before use or they will discolor the cream.

Wine and Cream Charlotte

Makes 12 pieces

335 calories per serving
Preparation time: about 1½ hours
Baking time: about 12 minutes
Cooling time: 5-6 hours

| For the outside sponge: |
| 4 eggs, separated |

3 tbs. warm water
½ cup honey
½ tsp. vanilla extract
Pinch salt
¾ cup wheat flour
½ cup buckwheat flour
Butter to grease
2⅓ cups unsweetened rosehip pulp or currant jelly
For filling and decoration
1¼ tbs. gelatin
3 eggs, separated
100 grams honey
Grated rind of ½ lemon
Juice 1 lemon
1 cup dry white wine
2 tbs. orange liqueur
Pinch salt
2¾ cups cream
1¼ cup white grapes
1 tbs. chopped pistachio nuts

Preheat oven to 400°F. • Beat together the egg yolks, water and vanilla until creamy. • Beat the egg whites until stiff and add them to the mixture. • Sieve the wheat flour and buckwheat flour over the mixture and stir all the ingredients thoroughly. • Line a Swiss roll pan with wax paper and grease it with butter. Spread the mixture evenly over the pan and bake for about 12 minutes. • After baking turn the sponge out onto a clean sheet of wax paper, remove the used sheet (if necessary by brushing the paper with a little cold water) and spread the sponge with rose hip pulp or currant jelly. Immediately roll up the sponge, with the help of the paper, to form a Swiss roll and allow to cool. • For the filling, dissolve the gelatin in cold water and leave to stand according to the instructions on the packet. • Beat together the egg yolks, ½

cup honey, lemon rind, lemon juice and white wine until creamy. • Stir a little of the mixture into the gelatin. Now return this to the rest of the mixture, stirring continuously. • Add the brandy and orange liqueur and leave the mixture to set in the refrigerator. • Beat the egg whites, salt and half the cream until very stiff. As soon as the mixture begins to set, stir in the cream. Leave to cool in the refrigerator for a few minutes but do not allow to set completely. • Meanwhile, cut the Swiss roll into ½ in. thick slices. Line a round bowl with them and spoon in the cream, smooth the surface and leave to set completely. • Before serving beat the rest of the cream until stiff and sweeten with the remaining honey. Spoon this into a piping bag with a star-shaped nozzle. • Wash and dry the grapes, halve

them and remove the seeds. • Turn the charlotte out onto a serving plate and pipe the cream around the edge. Decorate this with grapes and pistachio nuts.

Tip: Any remaining Swiss roll can be served separately.

Blackforest Cake

Makes 16 pieces

370 calories per serving
Preparation time: about 1½ hours
Cooling time: 12 hour-overnight

For the dough:
2 oz. milk chocolate
6 eggs, separated
4 tbs. warm water
1¼ cup honey
Pinch salt
1 cup wheat flour
½ cup buckwheat flour

1 tsp. baking powder

2 tsp. carob (locust-beans) powder.

1 cup freshly ground almonds

Butter to grease

Graham cracker crumbs to line baking pan

1 jar (about 1½ lbs. fruit weight) cherries, sour unsweetened

3 cups cream

2 tbs. honey

½ tsp. vanilla extract

3 liqueur glasses kirsch

6 oz. milk chocolate

G rate the chocolate finely and put to one side. • Preheat the oven to 350°F. • Beat together the egg yolks and water until creamy. Add the honey and continue to beat until the mixture is very light and creamy. • Beat the egg whites and salt until stiff and add to the mixture. • Mix together the wheat flour, buckwheat flour, baking powder and carob and sieve over the mixture. Add the ground almonds and grated chocolate and thoroughly mix together all the ingredients. • Line an 11 in. spring-release pan with wax paper. Grease the base of it only with butter, so that the dough will rise evenly, and sprinkle with graham cracker crumbs. • Spoon in the dough mixture and bake on a lower shelf of the oven for 50-60 minutes. • Allow to cool for a few minutes before turning out onto a wire rack. Remove the wax paper (by brushing with a little cold water if necessary) and leave to cool overnight. • The following day, drain the cherries and keep the juice for future use. • Cut the cake twice horizontally. Beat the cream until stiff, add the honey and vanilla. Put 3 tablespoons into a piping bag with a star-shaped nozzle and leave in the refrigerator. • Put to one side 16 cherries for later decoration and add the remainder to a third of the cream. • Sprinkle the layers of sponge with kirsch. • Spread one layer with the cherry cream. Cover this with the second layer and spread half of the remaining cream onto this. Cover with the third layer and spread the rest of the cream on this. Place the cake in the refrigerator. • Grate the chocolate into small, curly flakes with a knife; sprinkle over the cake. • Decorate each of the 16 slices with a cream rosette and a cherry. Do not allow to stand long before serving as the chocolate and cherries may discolor the cream.

Buttercream Cake

Makes 12 pieces

550 calories
Preparation time: about 2 hours
Baking time: (per layer) 20-30 minutes

For the light sponge:
6 eggs
2 tbs. vanilla extract
1 cup honey
1½ cups wheat flour
Butter to grease
For the dark sponge:
6 eggs
3 tbs. warm water
Pinch salt
1 cup honey
1½ cups wheat flour
3 oz. milk chocolate
Butter to grease
For filling and decoration:
1⅓ cup butter

3 egg whites

Pinch salt

1 cup honey

1 egg

3 tbs. soybean milk

6 tbs. strawberry jam (made with honey or fructose)

½ cup flaked almonds

6 strawberries

To make the light sponge mixture, beat together the eggs, water, salt and vanilla until creamy. Add the honey and continue to beat until the mixture is light and creamy. • Preheat oven to 400°F. • Mix in the wheat flour to the egg and vanilla cream. Line an 11 in. diameter spring-release pan with wax paper. Grease the base only, to ensure that the dough will rise evenly. • Bake on a lower shelf of the oven for 20-30 minutes. Leave to cool on a wire rack overnight.

• To make the dark sponge follow the instructions as above but melt the chocolate in a double boiler and, when cool, add it to the mixture at the same time as the flour. Bake as above and leave to cool. • Cut each base in half horizontally. Divide each layer of sponge into four concentric rings of equal width, which will be rearranged later. • To ensure that the rings are cut to the same corresponding width in each layer it is probably easier to use a stencil for cutting. • For the filling, cream the butter until foamy. • Beat the egg whites and salt until stiff, add ½ cup of the honey, stirring in thoroughly. • Whisk together the rest of the honey and the egg with an electric mixer at maximum speed for about 30 seconds. Now add the soybean and continue to whisk for 2-3 minutes until the mixture is light and creamy. Mix in the

egg whites and creamed butter. Place a third of this cream in the fridge. • Strain the strawberry jam and add it to the cream, cool for a few minutes. • Now make four new cake layers by placing alternate light and dark sponge rings inside each other. Spread one layer with some of the cream. Place a second layer of rings on top of this so that the colored sponges alternate. Build up the remaining two layers of sponge and cream in this way. • Spread two-thirds of the light colored cream over the top and edge of the cake and place it in the refrigerator. • Melt the chocolate on a low heat and allow to cool slightly before adding to the rest of the buttercream. Put into a piping bag with a star-shaped nozzle. • Roast the flaked almonds in a dry frying pan until golden yellow and sprinkle on the edge of the cake. • Decorate

each of the 12 slices with a chocolate cream rosette and a strawberry half. Serve immediately or keep in the refrigerator until required.

Strawberry Cream Sponge Pyramid

Makes 12 pieces

420 calories per serving
Preparation time: about 45 minutes
Baking time: about 35 minutes

For the dough

4 eggs, separated

4 tbs. warm water

1½ cups honey

Pinch salt

1½ cups wheat flour

1 cup freshly ground almonds

Butter to grease

For filling and decoration

| 3¼ cups strawberries |
| 4 tbs. maraschino liqueur |
| 3 tbs. strawberry jam (made with honey or fructose) |
| 3 cups cream |
| 2 tbs. maple syrup |
| ½ tsp. vanilla extract |
| 1 tbs. chopped pistachio nuts |

Preheat oven to 350°F. • Beat together the egg yolks, honey and water until very creamy. • Beat the egg whites and salt until very stiff and add this to the egg yolk mixture. Stir in the flour and the almonds. • Line a 10 in. diameter spring-release pan with wax paper. Grease the base only so that the dough will rise evenly. • Spoon in the mixture and bake in the middle of the oven for about 35 minutes. Allow to cool slightly, place on a wire rack and remove the wax paper. Leave to cool completely. • Wash and hull the strawberries. Cut a third of them into pieces. • Cut the cake twice horizontally, sprinkle two of the layers with maraschino liqueur. Cover one of these layer with jam and place the second on top. • Beat the cream until stiff, add the maple syrup and the vanilla. Mix half of this with the strawberry pieces and heap onto the cake to form a dome shape. • Now cut the third cake layer once from the center to the edge so that it can be shaped into a dome. Place this on top of the strawberry cream and press down along the edge. • Decorate with the remaining cream, using a spoon or piping bag, and cover with the rest of the strawberries and pistachio nuts.

Rice, Wine Cream and Marzipan Wedding Cake

Makes 40 pieces

395 calories per serving
Preparation time: about 5 hours
Baking time: in total about 1½ hours

Cooling time: about 3 hours

For the dough:

4 cups milk

Pinch salt

Grated rind of ½ lemon

1 cup natural shortgrain rice

¾ cup butter

1¾ cups honey

6 eggs

1 tsp. maize flour

Pinch baking powder

2 cups very finely ground almonds

For the filling:

white gelatin

¾ cup butter

6 egg yolks

Juice 2 lemons

½ cup dry white wine

Grated rind of 1 lemon

2 cups honey

2 tbs. cognac or armagnac

2 cups cream

Salt

For the decoration:

5⅔ cups almonds

4 cups honey

2-3 tbs. rose water

A few drops beetroot or spinach juice for coloring

Put the milk, salt and lemon rind into a saucepan and bring to a boil. Add the rice, re-boil, stirring continuously and simmer on a low heat for about 45 minutes. Drain in a sieve. • Cream the butter and add the honey, eggs and spices. • Mix together the wheat flour and baking powder and stir it into the rice. Mix in the almonds. • Preheat oven to 400°F. • Line 3 spring-release pans of 11 in, 22 in., and 7 in. diameters with baking foil. Spoon the mixture into each pan and bake each for 15-20 minutes. If you have room

you can bake two bases at the same time. • Leave the cake layers to cool on a wire rack. • For the filling, dissolve the gelatin according to the instructions on the packet. • Gently melt the butter and leave to cool until lukewarm. Place the egg yolks, lemon juice, wine, lemon rind, honey and cream in a basin. Place this in a saucepan of hot water. Whisk all the ingredients until creamy and thick. • Mix the gelatin in the cream, and whisk in the butter. Now place the bowl in cold water and continue to whisk until the mixture is cold. Add cognac or armagnac to taste and leave to cool in the refrigerator. • Beat the cream until stiff. Just before the mixture sets stir in the cream. • Cover each base with the mixture and place them on top of each other in tiers. Leave to stand in a cool place. • Scald the almonds with

boiling water, peel and dry. Work into a marzipan with the honey and rose water in a mixer. • Dye a small amount of marzipan green with the spinach juice. • Place the rest of the marzipan between sheets of baking foil and roll out thinly. Cut to cover the surface of each tier of the cake. • Roll out some of the pink marzipan to six very thin ribbons. Braid two ribbons together and place around the base of each tier. • Roll out the rest of the pink marzipan thinly and cut out small, round shapes. • To make the roses, form a small marzipan cone and place a few of the small circles around it. Press gently together and carefully bend the petal edges outwards. Decorate the cake top with the roses. • Cut the leaves out of the green marzipan and arrange around the roses.

Tip: The marzipan coating and the roses will stick better if they are coated with a little whisked egg white. • This wedding cake can also be prepared with the buckwheat sponge mixture as for Blueberry Cream Cake.

Honey Ice Cake with Walnuts

Makes 16 pieces

385 calories per serving
Preparation time: about 2 hours
Baking time: about 4 hours
Freezing time: about 6 hours

For the base:
4 egg whites
Pinch salt
1 cup honey
1 tsp. lemon juice
1¼ cups walnuts, freshly ground

1 tsp. carob (locust-beans) powder
For the rest:
2 cups walnuts
2 eggs
2 egg yolks
Pinch salt
1 cup honey
¼ tsp. vanilla extract
1 tsp. cinnamon powder
4 tbs. brandy
2 tbs. creme de cacao
3 cups cream
2 oz. milk chocolate

Preheat oven to 210°F. • Line a baking sheet with wax paper and draw a 10 in. diameter circle on it, using a circular baking pan. • Beat the egg whites and salt until stiff. Add the honey and continue to beat until the mixture is very creamy. Now add the lemon juice, walnuts and carob. Stir in thoroughly. • Put the mixture in a piping bag with a large nozzle and pipe into the circle in spiral lines, completely filling the circle. • Place the baking sheet in the middle of the oven and bake for 4 hours. Leave the oven door slightly open, using a wooden spoon if necessary, in order to let the moisture escape. • After baking remove the paper (if necessary by brushing with a little cold water) and allow the base to cool on a wire rack. • Put to one side 16 walnuts for decoration and chop the rest finely. • Whisk together the eggs, egg yolks and salt in a basin. Place the basin in a saucepan of hot water and add the honey, whisking continuously. Stir in the vanilla and cinnamon powder and continue to whisk until the mixture is thick and creamy. The water must not boil, otherwise the eggs will curdle. Take the bowl out of the saucepan and place in cold water. Add the brandy and creme de cacao and continue to whisk until completely cold. If the ingredients are not thoroughly whisked together the liqueur might separate out when frozen. • Beat 2 cups of cream until stiff and fold into the mixture. Stir in the walnuts. Encase the nut meringue base with the sides of a circular baking pan and fill with the cream. • Put the cake in the freezer and leave for about 6 hours. • Just before the cake is ready melt the chocolate in a small saucepan over a low heat and dip the walnuts in it. Place them on a close mesh wire rack and allow to harden. • Beat the remaining cream until stiff and spoon it into a piping bag with a star-shaped nozzle. • Remove the baking pan from the cake and decorate each of the

16 slices with a cream rosette and chocolate walnut.

Christmas Fruit Loaves

355 calories per serving
Soaking time: 3-4 hours
Preparation time: about 1 hour
Rising time: at least 2 hours
Baking time: about 1½ hours

2½ cups dried pears
1¼ cups dried pitted plums
¾ cups dried apples
¾ cups dried apricots
½ cup raisins
½ cup red wine
1½ cups warm water
1 cup figs
1 cup almonds
1 cup hazelnuts
2 tbs. candied lemon peel
¼ cup candied orange peel
3½ cups wheat flour
3½ cups rye flour
¼ cup fresh yeast
1-2 tsp. cinnamon powder
Pinch each aniseed, allspice and fennel, freshly ground
2 tbs. honey
Pinch salt
Juice and grated rind of 1 orange
Wheat flour for dusting and shaping
Butter to grease and brush

Wash the dried fruits in hot water, dry and dice. Place in a bowl, cover with the wine and warm water and leave to stand, covered for 3-4 hours. • Wash the figs in hot water, dry, remove stalks and dice. • Scald the almonds with boiling water, immerse in cold water and remove the skins. Leave to dry on a kitchen towel. Split ½ cup of the almonds and put to one side. Coarsely chop the remainder with the hazelnuts. • Dice the orange and lemon peel finely. • Mix together the wheat flour and rye flour, make a well in the center and crumble the yeast into it. Sprinkle with the dried spices. Work the center into a dough with a little of the water from the dried fruits and some flour from the edge. Cover and leave to stand in a warm draft-free place until it has risen and has started to bubble. • Sieve the soaked fruits, collecting the juice. Add sufficient water to the juice to make 1 cup of liquid. If it has gone cold gently heat up again until lukewarm. • Now add the honey, salt, 1 cup liquid, orange juice and rind to the dough. Knead all the ingredients to a smooth dough. Add a little more water if needed. Beat the dough until it leaves the sides of the bowl and starts to bubble. • Add the soaked fruits and figs, hazelnuts, almonds, lemon and orange peel and thoroughly mix all these into the dough. Sieve a little flour over it and leave to stand in a warm place until it has doubled in size. Depending on the room temperature it will take 1–1½ hours. • Preheat oven to 350°F. • Sprinkle work surface with flour. Knead the dough again and form into two oval shaped loaves. Decorate with the split almonds. • Grease a baking tray with butter, place the loaves on it some distance apart, and leave to stand for about 15 minutes. • Bake on a low shelf for about 1½ hours. Brush with a little butter from time to time. After baking brush once more with butter and leave to cool on a wire rack. • Keep for about 1 week before eating.

Tropical Fruit Butter Loaf

370 calories per serving
Preparation time: about 45 minutes
Baking time: about 1 hour
Rising time: at least 1½ hours

4 cups wheat flour
¼ cup fresh yeast
1 cup lukewarm milk
1 cup honey
1 cup soft butter
2 eggs
½ tsp. salt
1 vanilla pod
Grated rind of ½ lemon
Pinch each cardamon and coriander, freshly ground
2 pinches each cinnamon powder and mace
1 cup dried figs
1⅓ cups dates
⅓ cup dried bananas
¼ dried papayas
2 tbs. sesame seeds
½ cup coarsely chopped pistachio nuts
Wheat flour to roll out and shape
Butter to grease
½ cup butter for brushing

Pour the flour into a bowl and make a well in the center and crumble the yeast into it. Add a little milk and honey and some of the flour and knead to a smooth dough. Cover and leave to stand for 15-20 minutes, until it has risen and is starting to bubble. • Chop the butter into small pieces and add to the dough with the remaining milk, remaining honey, eggs and salt. • Slit the vanilla pod lengthways and remove the pulp. Add this, with the cardamon, coriander, mace and cinnamon powder, to the dough and knead all the ingredients to a smooth dough. • Beat until the dough leaves the sides of the bowl and starts to bubble. Cover and leave to stand for 30 minutes, until it has doubled in size. • Meanwhile, remove the stalks from the figs and dice them finely. Pit and dice the dates. Dice the bananas and papayas and mix all the fruit together with the sesame seeds and pistachios. • Knead the dough again on a lightly floured work surface. Work the fruit mixture into it and roll out to a thick oval. Fold the dough lengthways into the middle so that the bottom edges overlap a little. Lightly press together. • Grease a baking sheet with butter. Place the loaf on it and leave to stand for 20-30 minutes. • Preheat oven to 400°F. • Bake the loaf on a low shelf of the oven for about 1 hour. Melt the butter and brush the loaf, while still hot, until it will not absorb any more.

Tip: The empty vanilla pods can be used to make a vanilla essence. Put them in a small, dark bottle and fill with brandy, rum or rye whisky. Seal the bottle and leave to stand for at least 1 week. • This essence will be so strong that only a drop or two will ever be needed at once. Also if it has to be topped up with new pods always use the same alcohol as before. These should never be mixed.

Fruit Cakes and Cream Cakes

Even if you prefer to be invited to a friend's for a dinner rather than cake and coffee, your mouth still starts watering at the first appearance of cakes covered in strawberries, cherries, apples or plums. But these are not the only fruit pastries you will find in this section. Wait until you see the juicy mixture of apricots and almonds in a cheesecake, or a cake with gooseberry topping and marzipan, blackberry cake made with yogurt, the delicate mixture of pecan nuts and orange in yet another cake and subtle tastes of banana and pineapple in a nut cake, and particularly the blend of pears and walnuts in another! And the list seems to get endless as you discover pears and pumpernickel, apple strudel, hazelnuts mixed with barley and gooseberries, etc. etc. etc.!

Indeed you will find a recipe to suit each season of the fruit calendar and yet all with one thing in common: the delicious aroma of whole grain wheat and sun-ripened nuts and fruits, all carefully mixed and cooked with eggs, honey, cream, butter and a variety of appetizing and healthy ingredients.

Apple Date and Coconut Cake

Makes 12 pieces

475 calories per serving
Preparation time: about 1 hour
Cooling time: about 45 minutes
Baking time: about 1 hour

For the dough:
½ cup butter
1 cup honey
1 egg
1 egg yolk
2 pinches vanilla extract
Pinch salt
1¾ cups wheat flour
¼ cup buckwheat flour
1 cup grated coconut
In addition:
½ cup whole grain biscuits with honey
Butter to grease
For the filling:

1 cup dried dates
3¼ cups baking apples
Juice 1 lemon
4 eggs, separated
1 cup honey
2 tbs. rum
Pinch salt
½ cup cream
1 cup grated coconut

Beat together the butter, honey, egg, egg yolk, vanilla and salt until very creamy. • Add the wheat flour, buckwheat flour and grated coconut. Mix all the ingredients thoroughly and knead into a smooth dough. Wrap in foil and cool in a refrigerator for about 45 minutes. • Preheat oven to 400°F. • Break up the whole grain biscuits and put in a plastic bag and crumble them with a rolling pin. • Grease an 11 in. diameter spring-release pan and line with some of the crumbs. • Roll out the dough and press down firmly into the baking pan, forming a 1½ in. high edge. Line the inside of the edge with a strip of foil, prick the base with a fork and bake on the middle shelf for 10-15 minutes. • Meanwhile, pit and dice the dates. Wash and peel the apples and cut them into 8 slices. Sprinkle with lemon juice. • Beat together the egg yolks, honey, remaining lemon juice and rum until very creamy. • Beat the egg whites and salt with the cream until stiff. Add this to the mixture with the grated coconuts and the rest of the whole grain crumbs. Now mix all the ingredients well together. • Remove the base from the oven and take out the foil. • Pile the apples over the base, cover with the dates and spread the mixture over them. • Bake in the middle of the oven for 40-50 minutes. If the surface begins to brown too quickly cover it with foil. • Allow the cake to cool before placing on a wire rack.

Apple Sponge Cake

Makes 12 pieces

325 calories per serving
Preparation time: about 45 minutes
Baking time: about 50 minutes

⅔ cup butter
1 cup honey
Pinch salt
½ tsp. cinnamon powder
2 eggs
1¼ cup wholewheat flour
½ cup fine cornflour
1½ tsp. baking powder
½ cup linseeds
1 cup finely ground almonds
Butter to grease

Graham cracker crumbs to line baking pan

4 cups cooking apples

Juice 1 lemon

⅓ cup raisins

⅓ cup halved almonds

Beat the butter with the honey, salt and cinnamon until it is very creamy, gradually adding the eggs. • Mix the wholewheat flour and cornflour with the baking powder and stir into the mixture with the linseed and the ground almonds. • Preheat the oven to 350°F. • Carefully grease an 11 in. diameter spring-release pan with the butter and line with the graham cracker crumbs. • Fill with the mixture and level the surface. • Peel, halve and core the apples. Cut wedges into the round surface of the fruit several times quite close, but do not cut right through the fruit. Brush immediately with lemon juice. • Now lay the apple halves onto the mixture in a circular pattern. Press them down lightly. • Wash the raisins in a sieve under hot water, rub them dry in a cloth and sprinkle them over the apples with the almond pieces. • Bake the cake on the low shelf of the hot oven for about 50 minutes, allow to cool for a while in the pan, and then cool on a wire rack.

Apricot and Raspberry Flan

Makes 12 pieces

265 calories per serving
Preparation time: about 45 minutes
Cooling time: about 30 minutes
Baking time: 20-25 minutes

1½ cups wholewheat flour

½ cup finely ground millet

⅓ cup freshly ground almonds

Pinch salt

1 egg

Grated rind of ½ lemon

5 tbs. honey

½ cup chilled butter

Butter to grease

Graham cracker crumbs to line quiche pan

1⅓ cup raspberries, fresh or frozen unsweetened

3¼ cups ripe apricots

½ cup water

½ cup dry white wine

½ cup heavy cream

1 tbs. finely chopped pistachios

Mix the wheatflour and the millet with the almonds and the salt, and make a well in the center. Put into this the egg, the lemon rind and 3 tablespoons honey. Cut the butter into small pieces and dot around the flour. • Chop all the ingredients with two knives until they are mixed together like crumbs, then knead very quickly to a smooth dough. Make this into a ball, wrap in plastic wrap, and allow to cool for about 30 minutes in the refrigerator. • Grease an 11 in. diameter quiche pan with the butter and line with the graham cracker crumbs. • Preheat the oven to 400°F. • Press the dough flat into the pan and prick the bottom several times with a fork, so that no bubbles arise during baking. • Place the tart on the middle shelf of the hot oven and bake for 20-25 minutes, until well-cooked, but not too dark. • Turn out immediately onto a wire rack and allow to cool. • Dissolve the gelatin in a little cold water. Rinse the raspberries quickly under cold water, pat them dry very thoroughly, and only then hull them. If using frozen raspberries, allow to defrost. • Wash the apricots, pour boiling water over them and allow to soak for 1-2 minutes. Cool them with the cold water, skin, halve and pit. Cut the fruit halves into equal slices. • Makes circles of alternating apricot slices and raspberries on the cooled flan base, laying the apricot slices over each other like roof tiles. Set aside 12 especially nice raspberries for decoration. • Warm the water with the white wine and the remaining honey, but do not allow to boil. Stir the gelatin into the liquid to dissolve. Allow to cool until it is just beginning to gel. • Pour the gelatin over the fruit, smooth it over, taking care that none runs over the pastry-edge. Allow to set. • Before serving, whip the cream until stiff and put into a piping bag with a star-shaped nozzle. • Mark the surface of the flan into 12 pieces and pipe a thick rosette of cream onto each one. Decorate these with the reserved raspberries and the chopped pistachios. Serve the flan as soon as possible.

Sponge Roll with Strawberry Cream

Makes 12 pieces

240 calories per serving
Preparation time: about 1 hour
Baking time: 10-12 minutes

For the sponge:

5 eggs, separated

5 tbs. warm water

1 cup honey

Pinch salt

¾ cup fine wholemeal flour

½ cup buckwheat flour

2 pinches baking powder

For the filling:

1⅓ cup ripe strawberries

2 cups heavy cream

1 tsp. maraschino

Preheat the oven to 400°F. • Line a baking tray with wax paper, folding it up high at the sides of the tray. • Beat the egg yolks with the water and about 1 cup honey until it is thick and creamy. • Beat the egg whites with the salt until stiff enough to show the imprint of a knife. Pile it on top of the yolk mixture. • Mix the 3 flours with the baking powder, heap onto the egg whites and fold everything lightly together. • Smooth the mixture onto the paper and bake on the middle shelf of the hot oven for 10-12 minutes. • In the meantime lay a sheet of wax paper on the work surface. • Turn the sponge onto the surface, brush the paper with cold water and remove immediately. Replace the baking tray onto the sponge and allow to cool. As the moisture cannot escape, the sponge will remain soft so that it can easily be rolled up later. • Rinse the strawberries under cold water and pat dry thoroughly. Set aside 12 especially nice ones, hull and halve the others. • Whip the cream until stiff, sweeten with the remaining honey, and flavor with the maraschino. Put about 3 tablespoons in a piping bag with a star-shaped nozzle. • Mix the remaining cream gently with the strawberry halves, spread onto the surface of the sponge and roll it up from the long side. • Mark into 12 pieces on the top and crown each one with a rosette of cream with a strawberry on top.

Gooseberry Marzipan Cake

Makes 12 pieces

365 calories per serving
Preparation time: about 1 hour
Cooling time: about 45 minutes
Baking time: about 65 minutes

Cake ingredients:

1 cup wholewheat flour
½ cup buckwheat flour
1 cup freshly ground almonds
Pinch salt

Pinch cinnamon powder

1 egg yolk

1 cup honey

¼ lb. chilled butter

In addition you will need:

1 cup almonds

3⅓ cups gooseberries

3 tbs. rum

Butter for greasing

Graham cracker crumbs

3 egg whites

Pinch salt

Pinch cinnamon powder

2 egg yolks

2 tbs. maple syrup

3 tbs. coarse rolled oats

Mix the two flours with the almonds, salt and cinnamon and heap onto the work surface. Make a well in the center and put in the egg yolks with the honey, stirring together slightly. • Dot the butter in small pieces around the flour and quickly knead all the ingredients to a smooth dough. Roll this into a ball, wrap in plastic wrap and place in the refrigerator for about 45 minutes. • In the meantime blanch the almonds with boiling water, cool them in cold water and remove the brown skin. Dry them very thoroughly on a cloth. • Wash the gooseberries in cold water and pat them very dry. Top and tail them with scissors, and prick them a few times with a needle so that they will not burst during cooking. • Put the almonds through a grater twice, or reduce to very fine crumbs in the liquidizer. Stir with the honey and rum to a smooth marzipan paste. • Preheat oven to 400°F. • Grease an 11 in. diameter spring-release pan with butter and line with graham cracker crumbs. • Press the pastry into the pan with the hands, making a rim about 1½ in. high. Prick the base with a fork several times. • Pre-cook this base for about 15 minutes on the middle shelf of the hot oven. • Meanwhile, beat the egg whites and the salt to a snow stiff enough to hold the imprint of a knife. Flavor with the cinnamon and lemon rind. • Whisk the egg yolks with the maple syrup and fold gently into the egg whites with the rolled oats. Gradually work the marzipan paste into it. • Take the pastry base out of the oven and reduce the heat to 350°F. Leave the door open for a moment. • Spread the marzipan and egg mixture onto the slightly cooled base and distribute the gooseberries evenly onto it. • Place the cake back into the oven and cook for a further 50 minutes. If it should brown too quickly on top it may be covered with foil. • Allow the cake to cool in the pan for a while, then place on a wire rack to cool.

Redcurrant Flan

Makes 12 pieces

270 calories per serving
Preparation time: about 45 minutes
Cooling time: about 30 minutes
Baking time: about 40 minutes

For the pastry:

1¾ cups wholewheat flour

½ cup rolled oats with germ

¼ cup freshly ground hazelnuts

Pinch salt

2 pinches cinnamon powder

1 egg

½ cup honey

Grated rind of ½ lemon

½ cup butter

Butter for greasing

Graham cracker crumbs to line quiche pan

For the filling:

3⅓ cups redcurrants

5 egg whites

Pinch salt

1 tsp. lemon juice

4 tbs. honey

1 cup freshly ground hazelnuts

¼ cup rolled oats with germ

2 pinches cinnamon powder

Mix the wholewheat flour with the rolled oats, nuts, salt and cinnamon powder. • Stir the egg well with the honey, lemon rind and the butter. Work this mixture into the flour mixture, first stirring, then kneading. • Wrap the dough in plastic wrap and place in the refrigerator for about 30 minutes. • Preheat the oven to 40°F. • Grease an 11 in. diameter spring-release pan with the butter and line with the graham cracker crumbs. • Press the pastry into it, making a rim about 1½ in. high, and prick the bottom several times with a fork. • Bake this pastry base on the middle shelf of the hot oven for about 10 minutes. • In the meantime, wash the redcurrants, scrape off the stalks with a fork and dry off. • Beat the egg whites with the salt and lemon juice until stiff, and fold in the honey. • Mix the hazelnuts with the rolled oats and the cinnamon and fold into the egg whites with the redcurrants. • Spread this mixture onto the pastry base. Bake the flan on the low shelf of the oven for a further 30 minutes. Leave to cool in the pan for a short while, then cool on a wire rack.

Pear Flan with Walnuts

Makes 12 pieces

340 calories per serving
Preparation time: about 1 hour
Baking time: 45-55 minutes
Settling time: at least 1-2 days if possible

1½ cups oat groats
2 cups walnuts
⅔ cup butter
3 eggs
Pinch salt
1 cup pear juice concentrate
Juice and grated rind of 1 lemon
4 tbs. pear liqueur
1 tsp. cinnamon powder
Pinch ground cloves
½ cup buckwheat finely ground
1 cup wholewheat flour
1 tsp. baking powder
Butter for greasing
Graham cracker crumbs for lining quiche pan
2¼ cups ripe pears
3 tbs. cream

Put the oat groats in a dry frying pan and roast them lightly, stirring constantly. Then allow to cool on a large plate and grind to a medium texture.

Chop half of the walnuts coarsely and the other half finely. Melt ¼ lb. of the butter in a small saucepan on low heat, then remove from the heat. • Beat the eggs with the salt until very frothy, mixing in ½ cup pear juice concentrate, the lemon juice and rind, 2 tablespoons of pear liqueur, half the cinnamon and the cloves. • Mix the ground oats with the buckwheat and wholewheat flour, put in the baking powder and the finely chopped walnuts and stir together to make a dough. • Grease an 11 in. diameter spring-release pan with butter and line with graham cracker crumbs. • Put in the dough and smooth flat with a wet spatula. Put the pan to one side, so that the dough can expand while the topping is prepared. • Preheat the oven to 400°F. • Wash and core the pears and cut into equal slices.

Lay them in a circular pattern on the dough, overlapping each other like roof-tiles. • Allow the remaining butter to melt in a small saucepan and remove from heat. • Stir the remaining pear juice concentrate into the butter, together with the cream and the remaining pear liqueur. Flavor with the remaining cinnamon. Add the coarsely chopped walnuts, stir in well and distribute this mixture over the pears with two teaspoons, so that the pears are not completely covered. • Bake the cake on the low shelf of the hot oven for 45-55 minutes, until brown and crispy. If necessary, cover with foil during cooking. • Allow the cake to cool for a while in the pan, then place on a wire rack to cool. You must leave it for at least 1-2 days before cutting, under a cake net, to allow it to settle and the flavor to develop.

Plum Flan with Hazelnuts and Sesame

Makes 12 pieces

350 calories per serving
Preparation time: about 1 hour
Baking time: 40-50 minutes

1 cup sesame seeds
1 cup ricotta cheese
2 tbs. milk
Pinch salt
Grated rind of ½ lemon
1¼ cups honey
3 eggs, separated
4 tbs. oil
1½ cups wholewheat flour
½ cup finely ground millet
2 tsp. baking powder
4 cups plums
1 tsp. lemon juice
1 tsp. cinnamon powder
1 cup freshly ground hazelnuts

1 tbs. Slivovitz

Butter to grease

Graham cracker crumbs to line baking pan

2 tbs. maple syrup

Roast the sesame seeds lightly in a dry frying pan, stirring well, then allow to cool on a plate. • Put the ricotta into a bowl with the milk, add the salt, grated lemon rind and ½ cup honey. Stir everything well together, adding one egg yolk and the oil. • Mix the whole-wheat flour and the ground millet with the baking powder and ½ cup roasted sesame seeds. Add about half of this to the ingredients in the bowl. • Put the rest of the flour mixture onto the work surface, make a well in the center and put the mixture from the bowl into this. Working from the edge to the center, knead everything to a smooth dough and

allow to rest, covered, until the topping is ready. • Wash the plums in cold water and dry carefully. Then remove the stalks, halve and stone and cut into the plum halves a little way on one side, so that they do not contract during baking. • Whisk the egg whites with the lemon juice until stiff and add the remaining honey. Carry on whisking until very shiny and stiff. • Gently fold in the cinnamon powder, ground hazelnuts and the remaining sesame seeds. • Whisk the remaining egg yolks with the Slivovitz and stir into the beaten egg white. • Preheat the oven to 400°F. • Grease an 11 in. diameter spring-release pan with butter, and line with graham cracker crumbs. Press the dough flat into it. • Spread the hazelnut and sesame mixture on top of it and lay on the plums in a circular pattern. • Put the cake onto the low

shelf of the oven, and bake for 40-50 minutes. • Take the cake out of the oven and brush with maple syrup while still hot. • Leave the cake in the pan for a while to cool, and then put on a wire rack. Only cut it when it has cooled.

Variations: Plum Flan with Honey and Coconut Glaze. • Prepare the dough as in the previous recipe and leave to rest for a few minutes so that it can swell. Then put the dough into the prepared pan, press down smoothly and sprinkle it with a mixture of ¼ cup rolled oats and ¼ cup grated coconut (lightly roasted if you wish). Lay the plums closely together on this and bake the cake for about 30-40 minutes. Mix 1 cup honey with 2-3 tablespoons Slivovitz and about ¼ cup grated coconut. Spread this mixture onto

the hot cake, turn off the oven and let the glaze caramelize in there for about 5 minutes. Leave the cake in the pan for a short while, then leave to cool on a wire rack.

Apple Cake with Cream Glaze

Makes 20 pieces

235 calories per serving
Preparation time: about 50 minutes
Proving time: at least one hour
Baking time: 40-50 minutes

3 cups wholewheat flour
1 cup millet meal
½ cup buckwheat flour
¼ cup fresh yeast
¾ cup lukewarm milk
1 cup apple juice concentrate
1 egg
Pinch salt

| Grated rind of ½ lemon |
| 1 tsp. cinnamon powder |
| ¼ cup soft butter |
| Butter to grease |
| Graham cracker crumbs to line baking pan |
| ½ cup currants |
| 4 cups cooking apples |
| Juice 1-2 lemons |
| 1 cup flaked almonds |
| ½ cup cream |
| ½ cup heavy cream |

Mix the 3 flours in a bowl, make a well in the center and crumble the yeast into it. Make a small amount of dough in the center with some milk and a little flour from the edge. Leave to stand for 15 minutes. • Add to this the remaining milk with half the apple juice concentrate, the egg, salt, lemon rind and half the cinnamon. Dot the butter around the edge in small pieces. • Work all the ingredients to a smooth dough and beat it until it leaves the edge of the bowl and has bubbles in it. Leave to stand for at least 30 minutes, covered with a cloth, until it has clearly increased in size. • Grease a baking tray and line with graham cracker crumbs. • Knead the dough again, roll out onto the pan and leave to stand for a short while. • Preheat the oven to 400-425°F. • Wash the currants in hot water and rub well dry. • Peel, quarter and core the apples and cut into little chips. Mix immediately with lemon juice. Spread over the dough with the currants and almonds, and bake for 30-40 minutes on the middle shelf of the oven. • Whisk the cream with the remaining cinnamon, apple juice concentrate and the cream. Spoon onto the cake and brown lightly for 5-10 minutes.

Cherry Cake with Cashew Nuts and Crumble Topping

Makes 20 pieces

395 calories per serving
Preparation time: about 1½ hours
Standing time: at least one hour
Baking time: 35-45 minutes

| 3½ cups wholewheat flour |
| 1 cup millet meal |
| ¼ cup fresh yeast |
| ¾ cup lukewarm milk |
| ½ cup honey |
| 1 egg |
| Pinch salt |
| ½ tsp. vanilla extract |
| ¼ cup soft butter |
| ½ cup cashew nuts, chopped very finely |
| Butter to grease |
| Graham cracker crumbs to line baking pan |

For the topping:

| 7 cups sweet cherries |
| ¾ cup butter |
| ⅔ cup honey |
| Pinch salt |
| 1 egg yolk |
| 2½ cups wholewheat flour |
| ½ cup millet meal |
| ½ tsp. ground mace |
| ½ cup graham cracker crumbs |
| 1 cup cashew nuts, coarsely chopped |

Prepare the dough as described in the previous recipe, (Apple Cake with Cream Glaze), adding the cashew nuts with the spices. • Before leaving to stand for the third time, roll out the pastry onto a greased baking tray lined with graham cracker crumbs, and leave to stand for a few minutes. • Preheat the oven to 400-425°F. • Wash and dry the cherries, re-

move the stalks and pits. • Stir together the butter, honey, salt and egg yolk. • Mix both the flours with the mace, stir part of it into the butter mixture and rub in the rest to resemble breadcrumbs. • Sprinkle the dough with the graham cracker crumbs. • Mix the cherries with the cashew nuts, distribute over the dough and sprinkle with the crumble topping. • Place the baking tray immediately on the middle shelf of the hot oven and bake the cake for 35-40 minutes. • When cold, cut the cherry cake into slices.

Apricot Cheese Cake with Almonds

Makes 20 pieces

295 calories per serving
Preparation time: about 1 hour
Proving time: at least 1 hour
Baking time: 45-40 minutes

| 3½ cups wholewheat flour |
| 1 cup millet meal |
| ¼ cup fresh yeast |
| ¾ cup lukewarm milk |
| 1¼ cup honey |
| 3 eggs |
| Pinch salt |
| Grated rind of ½ orange |
| ¼ cup butter |
| ¼ cup candied orange peel, very finely chopped |
| Butter to grease |
| Graham cracker crumbs to line baking pan |
| 7 cups fresh apricots |
| ½ cup almonds |
| 1¾ cups full fat cream cheese |
| Juice 2 oranges |
| 1 tbs. apricot brandy |

Prepare the dough as for Apple Cake with Cream Glaze. Work in 1 cup honey, 1 egg and the candied peel just before leav-

ing to stand for the third time. •
Grease a baking pan and line
with crumbs. • Knead the dough
once more, roll out onto the pan
and leave to stand for a short
time. • Preheat the oven to
400°F. • Wash, dry, halve and pit
the apricots. Pour boiling water
over the almonds, skin them, dry
thoroughly and halve them. Beat
the cream cheese with the remaining egg and ½ cup honey,
and flavor with the juice of 1 orange and the apricot brandy. •
Spread onto the dough and lay
the apricots close together on top
of it. • Lay 1 almond half in each
apricot half and bake the cake
on the middle shelf of the oven
for 45-50 minutes. • Stir the remaining honey with the leftover
orange juice, brush onto the fruit
and allow to cool.

Blackberry Cake with Yogurt Cream

Makes 12 slices

430 calories per serving
Preparation time: about 1 hour
Baking time: 30-40 minutes
Time to cool and become firm:
about 1 day

For the cake:
4 eggs, separated
2 tbs. warm water
1 cup honey
Grated rind of ½ orange
Pinch salt
1½ cup wholewheat flour
½ cup almonds, freshly ground
½ tsp. baking powder
Butter to grease
For the filling and decoration:
3¼ cups blackberries, fresh or frozen unsweetened
3 tsp. white gelatin

3 eggs, separated
1¼ cups honey
Juice of 1 orange
Grated rind of ½ orange
Pinch ground ginger
2¼ cups creamy plain yogurt
2 tbs. raspberry liqueur
⅔ cup blackberry jam without added sugar
Pinch salt
2 cups heavy cream
½ cup flaked almonds

For the cake, beat the egg
yolks with the water, honey
and orange rind until pale and
creamy. • Preheat the oven to
350°F. • Whisk the egg whites
with the salt until stiff and pile
onto the egg yolks. • Mix the
flour with the ground almonds
and the baking powder, sift onto
the egg whites and fold gently
together. • Line the base of an
11 in. spring-release pan with

wax paper and brush with butter.
Immediately bake the sponge in
it on the low shelf of the heated
oven. • Leave for a while in the
pan, then tip onto a wire rack,
remove the wax paper, and leave
the sponge to cool at least until
the next day; it will be easier to
cut then. • For the filling, wash
the blackberries briefly in cold
water and drip dry or pat them
dry. Allow frozen berries to thaw,
and then to drip thoroughly. •
Dissolve the gelatin in a little cold
water. • Beat the egg yolks with
the honey, orange juice and rind
and the ginger until frothy. Mix
the gelatin in a small saucepan
with the raspberry liqueur on a
low heat. Allow to cool slightly,
stirring it, then mix in some
yogurt and beat this into the rest
of the yogurt. Place in the refrigerator to set. • Cut through
the sponge cake once horizontally. • Stir the jam until smooth

and spread on the lower sponge layer. • Whisk the egg whites with the salt until stiff and whip half the cream until very stiff. Fold both of these carefully into the yogurt cream as soon as it begins to set. Replace the cream in the refrigerator for a short while. • Close the rim of the spring-release pan around the sponge layer with jam on, and smooth half the yogurt cream onto it. • Place about three-quarters of the blackberries on the cream and cover with the remaining yogurt cream. Place the second sponge layer on top and allow the cream to set in the refrigerator. • Before serving, beat the remaining heavy cream until stiff and put about a third of it in a piping bag with a star-shaped nozzle. • Remove the rim of the pan and spread the sides of the cake with cream. • Decorate the sides of the cake with flaked al-monds, and the top with the cream from the piping bag and the remaining blackberries.

Orange and Pecan Nut Flan

Makes 12 pieces

405 calories per serving
Preparation time: about 1½ hours
Baking time: about 25 minutes
Cooling time: about 5 hours

For the pastry:
1¾ cups wholewheat flour
½ cup millet meal
½ cup pecan nuts, chopped very finely
1 egg
Pinch salt
Grated rind of ½ orange
½ cup maple syrup
⅔ cup chilled butter
Butter to grease

Graham cracker crumbs to line baking pan
Dried pulses for baking blind
For filling and decorating:
2 tbs. white gelatin
¾ cup butter
1 cup maple syrup
4 eggs
Grated rind and juice of 3 oranges
Juice of 1 lemon
3-4 tbs. orange liqueur
1¾ cups heavy cream
1-2 small oranges

Mix the wheatflour and millet with the pecan nuts, put onto the work surface and make a well in the center. Into this put the egg, salt, grated orange rind and maple syrup. Cut the chilled butter into small pieces and dot around the flour. Work all the ingredients quickly to a smooth dough. Shape into a ball, wrap in plastic wrap and place in the refrigerator for about 2 hours. • Grease an 11 in. diameter spring-release pan with butter and line with graham cracker crumbs. Preheat the oven to 400°F. • Press the short pastry flat into the prepared pan, making a 1½ in. high rim. Prick the base several times with a fork to prevent bubbles forming during baking. • Place a circle of wax paper inside the pastry and fill it with the pulses, so that the pastry rim cannot collapse during cooking. • Bake the cake for about 25 minutes on the middle shelf of the hot oven. • Remove the pulses and the wax paper and allow the pastry base to cool on a wire rack. • For the filling, dissolve the gelatin in a little cold water. • Cut the butter into very small flakes and whisk in a metal bowl with the maple syrup, eggs, rind and juice of the oranges and

For the shortcrust pastry, knead together the flours, the egg, salt, orange juice and rind, as well as the butter cut into small pieces. Wrap in plastic wrap and leave to cool for 2 hours in the refrigerator. • Preheat the oven to 400°F. • Grease a 10 in. diameter spring-release pan with butter and line with the graham cracker crumbs. • Press the pastry smoothly into it, making a rim about 1 in. high. Prick the base several times with a fork. • Cover the flan case with wax paper, fill with the dried pulses, and bake on the middle shelf of the hot oven for 20-25 minutes. • Remove the pulses and cool on a wire rack. • Dissolve the gelatin according to the instructions. • Mix the honey with the eggs and orange juice and rind in a bowl and place this in a saucepan of hot water and beat until thick and creamy. • Mix the gelatin into the creamy mixture. Place a bowl in a saucepan of cold water and beat until mixture has cooled. • Whip half of the cream until stiff and fold it gently into the mixture. • Fill the pastry base with the mixture and allow to set. • Afterwards whip the remaining cream until stiff and put into a piping bag. • Peel and segment the oranges as in the previous recipe, and decorate the flan with these, the cream and pistachios.

Peach Cake with Walnuts and Sesame

Makes 12 pieces

265 calories per serving

½ cup butter
½ cup honey
2 eggs
Pinch salt
Pinch cinnamon powder
Grated rind of ½ lemon
1¾ cups wholewheat flour
1 tsp. baking powder
½ cup sesame seeds
Butter to grease

the lemon. Now place the bowl in hot, but not boiling, water and beat the ingredients to a thick, foamy cream. You must not let it boil, otherwise the eggs will congeal. • Mix the gelatin in the creamy mixture, beating further. Flavor with the orange liqueur. • Place the bowl in a saucepan of cold water and cool the orange cream, beating very frequently, and allow to gel. • Shortly before it sets, pour the cream into the baked pastry case, smooth the surface and leave it in the refrigerator for about 3 hours until it is firm enough to cut. • Before serving whip the double cream until stiff and put into a piping bag with a star-shaped nozzle. • Peel the small oranges, removing all the white strings. Then care-fully segment the orange removing the pits. • Decorate the surface of the orange cream with rosettes of whipped cream and place the orange slices on top of these. • Bring the flan to the table as quickly as possible. Otherwise leave in the refrigerator until ready to serve.

Fine Orange Flan

Makes 12 pieces

305 calories per serving
Preparation time: about 1½ hours
Cooling time: about 5 hours
Baking time: 20-25 minutes

For the dough:
1½ cups millet meal
1 cup wholewheat flour
1 egg
Pinch salt
Juice and grated rind of ½ orange
⅔ cup chilled butter
Butter to grease
Graham cracker crumbs to line baking pan
Dried pulses for baking blind
For filling and decoration:
2 tbs. white gelatin
1¼ cups honey
4 eggs
Grated rind of 2 oranges
Juice of 3 oranges
1 cup heavy cream
1-2 small oranges
2 tsp. pistachios, freshly chopped

Graham cracker crumbs to line baking pan

½ cup walnuts, freshly chopped

2 cans (1 lb. each) peach halves, sweetened with honey or fructose

1-2 tsp. confectioners' sugar for dusting (optional)

Cut the butter into little flakes and stir until frothy with the honey and eggs. Flavor with the salt, cinnamon and grated lemon rind. • Mix the wholewheat flour with the baking powder and half the sesame seeds and stir gently into the liquid. • Preheat the oven to 400°F. • Grease a 10 in. diameter spring-release pan, and line it with the graham cracker crumbs. • Put in the mixture and smooth the top. • Mix the remaining sesame with the walnuts and sprinkle half of this onto the cake mixture. • Drain the peach halves and pat dry. Lay one half

with its round side up in the middle, cut the other halves into 2 or 3 slices and arrange around the peach half in a star-shaped pattern. • Sprinkle over the remaining sesame and walnut mixture, and bake the cake for 50-60 minutes on the middle shelf of the hot oven. • After a short cooling time, slide the cake onto a wire rack and allow to cool completely. • Before serving, sprinkle with the confectioners' sugar, if desired.

Banana Cake with Pineapple and Pistachios

Makes 12 pieces

320 calories per serving
Preparation time: about 45 minutes
Baking time: about 40 minutes

½ small pineapple (about 1 lb. 2 oz.)

1 liqueur glass rum

2½ cups wholewheat flour

¾ cup soft butter

1 cup honey

3 eggs

Pinch salt

Pinch each ground mace and ground ginger

1⅓ cups bananas

Juice of 1 lemon

1½ cups buckwheat flour

2 tsp. baking powder

¼ cup pistachios, coarsely chopped

Butter to grease

Graham cracker crumbs to line baking pan

2 oz. milk chocolate

Remove the pineapple leaves and hard part around the stalk, peel carefully and remove the hard core from the middle. Now cube the flesh of the fruit

and leave, covered, to soak with the rum. • Sieve the wheatflour and set the bran that is left on one side. • Beat the butter with the honey, eggs and spices until frothy. • Preheat the oven to 350-400°F. • Purée the bananas with the lemon juice and stir into the mixture. • Mix the wholewheat flour (without the bran) with the buckwheat and the baking powder. • Drain the pineapple pieces and add the pistachios and the bran. • Stir these and the flour into the mixture. • Grease an 11 in. diameter spring-release pan and line with graham cracker crumbs. • Smooth the mixture into it and bake on the lower shelf of the hot oven for 40 minutes. • Allow the cake to cool on a wire rack. • Melt the chocolate and, using a pointed knife, allow to run over the top of the cake in a zig-zag pattern.

Peach Cheesecake with Almond Croquant

Cut into 12 pieces

580 calories per serving
Preparation time: about 1½ hours
Cooling time altogether: about 2½ hours
Baking time altogether: about 2½ hours

For the pastry:
1¾ cups wholewheat flour, freshly ground
½ cup millet meal
¼ cup almonds, freshly ground
Pinch salt
1 egg
3 tbs. honey
½ cup butter
Butter for greasing
Graham cracker crumbs for sprinkling

For filling and decoration:
5 ripe peaches
Juice of 1 lemon
8-10 large sweet cherries
2¼ cups ricotta cheese
1¾ cups cream
1¾ cups honey
3 eggs
½ cup millet meal
Pinch salt
1 cup heavy cream
½ tsp. vanilla extract
2 tbs. almonds, freshly ground
¼ cup butter
1 tbs. almond liqueur
3 tbs. heavy cream
1 cup flaked almonds

Mix the wheat and millet flours with the almonds and salt and put onto the work surface. Make a well in the center and put into this the egg with the honey. Cut the butter into very small pieces and place around the edge of the flour. • Using two knives, chop all the ingredients to a crumbly mixture, then knead quickly with the hands to a smooth dough. • Wrap this in plastic wrap and place in the refrigerator for about 30 minutes. • Preheat the oven to 400°F. • Grease an 11 in. diameter spring-release pan with butter, and sprinkle with graham cracker crumbs. • Press the pastry flat onto the base, and prick several times with a fork. Bake blind for about 15 minutes on the middle shelf of the hot oven. • Remove the pastry base from the oven and allow to cool. • In the meantime, pour boiling water over the peaches, and leave them in it for a few seconds. • Cool the fruit down quickly with cold water, skin, halve and stone. • Brush the halves immediately with lemon juice, so that they do not go brown. • Wash the cherries in cold water, dry, remove the stalks and stone. • Beat the ricotta well with the cream, 1¼ cups honey and the eggs. Add the millet and the salt and fold in carefully. • Heat the oven again to 400°F. • Whisk the heavy cream with the vanilla until stiff and fold gently into the ricotta cream. • Sprinkle the ground almonds onto the baked base. • Put a cherry in each peach half and place on the almond layer with the cut side down. • Spoon the ricotta cream over it and smooth flat. • Place the cake immediately on the bottom shelf of the hot oven and bake for about 2 hours. Cover the surface with aluminum foil after 1 hour so that it does not brown. • Take the cake out of the oven and allow to cool. • Before you prepare the croquant topping, turn the oven to its highest setting, (if

possible, with heat from above).
• Melt the butter with the remaining honey by stirring in a wide pan. Pour in the almond liqueur with the heavy cream and the flaked almonds and, continuing to stir carefully, let it simmer gently until it begins to caramelize. • Spread it immediately onto the surface of the ricotta and bake for 8-10 minutes in the very hot oven, until golden brown. • Allow the cake to cool, then run a knife along between the cake and the pan, remove the rim and place the cake on a plate.

Swiss Pear and Walnut Flan

Cut into 8 pieces

470 calories per serving
Preparation time: about 45 minutes
Cooling time: about 30 minutes
Baking time: about 45 minutes

2¼ cups wholewheat flour, freshly ground
Pinch baking powder
½ cup walnuts, freshly ground
Pinch salt
5 tbs. honey
4 tbs. pear liqueur
2 eggs
½ cup butter
Butter for greasing
Graham cracker crumbs for sprinkling
3¼ cups pears
Juice of 1 lemon
½ cup walnuts, coarsely chopped
1 egg yolk
½ cup heavy cream
2 tbs. cream
Pinch cinnamon powder
1 tbs. pear juice concentrate

Sift out about 2 tablespoons bran from the wheatflour • Mix the remaining flour with the baking powder, nuts and salt, and make a well in the center. Put into this 2 tablespoons honey, 2 tablespoons pear li-

queur and 1 egg, and distribute the small pieces of butter over it. • Knead all the ingredients to a smooth dough. Wrap this in plastic wrap and leave to rest for 30 minutes in the refrigerator. • Preheat the oven to 400°F. • Grease a 10 in. diameter flan or pizza pan and sprinkle with graham cracker crumbs. Line it with the pastry and prick several times with a fork. Bake blind for about 10 minutes on the middle shelf of the hot oven. • In the meantime, peel the pears, core, cut into slices and drip lemon juice over them. • Remove the

baked flan case from the oven and arrange the pear slices very closely together in a circular pattern. • Spoon the chopped nuts and about 2 tablespoons honey over the pears and bake the flan for a further 10 minutes. • Beat the remaining egg to a light froth with the egg yolk, the rest of the honey, the cream, the cinnamon powder, the remaining pear liqueur and the pear juice concentrate, and fold in the bran. • Spoon this mixture over the pears and bake the flan for a further 15 minutes. Bring to the table while still warm.

Sesame and Nut Flan with Millet and Berry Cream

Cut into 12 pieces

295 calories per serving
Preparation time: about 1½ hours
Baking time: about 25 minutes
Cooling time: about 3 hours

For the pastry:
½ cup sesame seeds
1 cup peanuts, freshly peeled
2 cups wholewheat flour, freshly ground

1 egg
Pinch salt
1 tbs. honey
Grated rind of ½ lemon
½ cup chilled butter
Wheatflour for rolling out
2¼ lbs. pulses for baking blind
For the filling and decoration:
1 cup milk
Pinch salt
½ vanilla pod
½ cup millet meal
1 tbs. white gelatin
3 tbs. honey
1 glass (1 oz.) rum or arak
2¾ lbs. mixed berries
3 cups heavy cream
2-3 sprigs lemon balm

Lightly roast the sesame seeds in a dry pan, stirring well, and allow to cool on a plate. • Put the peanut kernels in a plastic bag and crush as finely as possible with a rolling pin. Mix with the wheatflour and sesame, pile onto the work surface and make a well in the center. • Put the egg, salt, honey and lemon rind into the well. • Cut the butter into little pieces, dot around the flour, cut the ingredients to a crumb texture and knead quickly to a smooth dough. Form into a ball, wrap in plastic wrap or a plastic bag, and place in the refrigerator for at least ½ hour. • Preheat the oven to 400°F. • Roll out the pastry thinly on a floured work surface and line an ungreased 11 in. diameter spring-release pan with it, making a 1½ in. high border. Prick the base several times with a fork, cover with wax paper and shake in the pulses. • Bake the pastry case on the middle shelf of the hot oven for 20-25 minutes. • Take out the pulses and paper, and allow the flan to cool on a wire rack. •

For the filling warm the milk in a saucepan with the salt. • Cut the vanilla pod open lengthways, scrape out the core and put into the milk together with the "empty" pod. Stir in the millet and let it come to a boil while continuing to stir. Turn down the heat and let the millet swell— very well covered—for about 30 minutes on the lowest heat. • In the meantime dissolve the gelatin according to the instructions on the packet. • Take the millet off the heat and stir in the honey and the gelatin in the mixture while still hot. Place in a large bowl, flavor with the rum or arak and allow to cool. • Meanwhile, wash the berries briefly in cold water, pat dry carefully and remove cores and stalks. Save a few especially nice ones for decoration. • Shortly before the mixture begins to set, whip about ⅔ of the cream until stiff, and fold in gently, together with the berries. • Spoon this mixture into the pastry case, level the surface and allow to set completely in the refrigerator. • Immediately before serving, whip the remaining cream until stiff and put into a piping bag with a star-shaped nozzle. Rinse the lemon balm under cold water, pat dry and pluck off the leaves. • Mark the flan surface into 12 pieces and decorate each with cream rosettes or spirals, berries and lemon balm leaves.

Apple Tart

Cut into 12 pieces

265 calories per serving
Preparation time: about 30 minutes
Cooling time: about 1 hour
Baking time: altogether 25 minutes

1¼ cups wholewheat flour

1 cup millet meal

½ cup almonds, freshly ground

Pinch salt

1 egg

4 tbs. honey

Grated rind of ½ lemon

⅔ cup chilled butter

Butter for greasing

Graham cracker crumbs for sprinkling

4 cups apples

2 tbs. apricot jam without added sugar (from the Health Food shop)

Mix the wheat and millet flour with the almonds and make a well in the center. • Put in the salt, egg, 1 tablespoon honey and the lemon rind. • Cut the butter into small pieces, sprinkle over the flour and chop everything to a crumb texture.

Then knead to a smooth dough with cooled hands. • Shape the dough into a ball, wrap in plastic wrap and allow to rest in the refrigerator for about 1 hour. • Preheat the oven to 475°F-500°F. • Grease a flan or tart dish or an 11 in. diameter spring-release pan and sprinkle with crumbs. • Line the pan with the pastry, making a rim about 1 in. high, and prick the base several times. • Peel the apples if you prefer and cut into thin slices, removing the core. • Lay the slices close to each other on the pastry in a star-shaped pattern, and coat with 1 tablespoon honey. • Put the tart immediately into the preheated oven on the middle shelf and bake for 20 minutes so that it is golden brown and crispy. • Warm the apricot jam with the remaining honey, spread on the tart and bake for a further 5

minutes. Afterwards allow to cool on a wire rack, or serve hot.

Swiss Flan with Plums and Yogurt

Cut into 12 pieces

380 calories per serving
Preparation time: about 1½ hours
Cooling time: about 1 hour
Baking time: 40-50 minutes

1½ cups wholewheat flour, freshly ground

1 cup millet meal

Pinch salt

1 cup honey

2 cups sour cream

¾ cup chilled butter

Butter for greasing

3 tbs. graham cracker crumbs

1 cup pecan nuts

4 cups plums

1 carton creamy plain yogurt

2 eggs

4 egg yolks

½ tsp. vanilla extract

2 tbs. yellow plum or apricot liqueur

Mix the wheat and millet flour with the salt and make a well in the center. Put in 1 tablespoon honey and 1¼ cups sour cream. • Cut the butter into small pieces and sprinkle over the flour. • Knead everything and keep cool, covered, for about an hour. • Grease a flan, pie or paella dish and sprinkle with about 1 tablespoon crumbs. • Chop 2 tablespoons pecan nuts and mix with the remaining crumbs. • Preheat the oven to 400°F–425°F. • Line the dish with the pastry and prick several times. Bake on the middle shelf for 15-20 minutes. • Meanwhile,

chop the remaining nuts coarsely. • Wash and pit the plums. • Beat the yogurt with the remaining sour cream and honey, the eggs and the egg yolks, and flavor with the vanilla and alcohol. • Sprinkle the crumb and nut mixture over the base, spread the yogurt mixture over it, and cover with the plums and the remaining nuts. • Bake again on the middle shelf for 25-30 minutes. Place the cake on a rack, or serve in the dish.

Farmhouse Apple Strudel

Cut into 12 pieces

365 calories per serving
Preparation time: about 1 hour
Resting time: about 1 hour
Baking time: 40-45 minutes

1½ cups wholewheat flour, freshly ground
1 cup buckwheat flour
½ tsp. salt
1 tsp. vinegar
5 tbs. sunflower oil
10-12 tbs. warm water
1 cup stale pumpernickel
1¼ cups hazelnuts, coarsely ground or very finely chopped
⅓ cup butter
⅔ cup raisins
4 cups cooking apples
Juice of 1 lemon
Wheatflour for rolling out
1¼ cups sour cream
1-2 tsp. ground cinnamon
5-6 tbs. apple juice concentrate
Butter for greasing

Sieve the flours and set aside about ¼ cup of the bran left behind. Put the flour mixture on the work surface with the rest of the bran and the salt and make a well in the center. • Pour the vinegar, sunflower oil and water into the well, and stir the ingredients from the middle out, then knead from the outside in. Carry on with this kneading for at least 10-15 minutes. • Shape the dough into a ball, put into a plastic bag and allow to rest for about an hour under a hot, dry pan (first boil water in it and then dry off), so that the flour can swell. • In the meantime break the pumpernickel into fine crumbs and mix with the hazelnuts and the bran. Heat ¼ cup butter in a frying-pan and roast this mixture lightly in it, stirring continuously. Remove the pan from the heat and allow the mixture to cool. • Wash the raisins in a sieve under hot water and rub dry carefully. • Peel, quarter and core the apples and cut into small pieces. Dribble the lemon juice over them immediately. • Cover the work surface with a large cloth and dust it with wheatflour. Roll out the pastry on it as thinly as possible. Put your hands under the pastry so that it can be pulled out wafer-thin. • Cut off any thick edges with scissors or a sharp knife. • Whip the sour cream lightly and spread on the pastry. • Then sprinkle the mixture of pumpernickel, nuts and bran onto the cream and spread with the apple pieces and raisins. • Dust everything with the cinnamon and let 3-4 tablespoons apple juice concentrate run over it in a thin stream. • Preheat the oven to 400°F. Fold the pastry over the filling on the short sides and roll up the pastry with the help of the cloth, starting with the long edge. • Grease a baking tray with butter and roll the strudel onto it straight off the cloth. • Melt the rest of the butter and brush the strudel with it. • Place the tray on

the middle shelf of the hot oven and bake for 40-45 minutes. • Then brush the strudel with the rest of the apple juice concentrate.

Creamy Strudel with Bananas and Raisins

Cut into 12 pieces

405 calories per serving
Preparation time: about 1 hour
Resting time: about 1 hour
Baking time: 45-55 minutes

2¼ cups wholewheat flour, freshly ground

1 cup buckwheat flour, freshly ground

½ tsp. salt

1 tsp. vinegar

5 tbs. sunflower oil

12-15 tbs. warm water

Oil for brushing

1 cup dried bananas

⅓ cup raisins
2 tbs. cognac or rum
¾ cup butter
1 cup honey
1 egg
1 egg yolk
Grated rind of ½ lemon
½ tsp. vanilla extract
Pinch ground cinnamon
2 cups ricotta cheese
1 cup cream
2 tbs. candied lemon peel, very finely diced
Wheatflour for rolling out
3 tbs. graham cracker crumbs
1 cup heavy cream

Sieve the wheat and buckwheat flour and set aside ¼ cup of the resulting bran. • Mix the sieved flour with the remaining bran again, make a well and put into it the salt, vinegar, sunflower oil and water, and stir from the middle out, then knead everything from the outside in to make a smooth dough. • Shape into a ball, brush thinly all over with oil and place in a plastic bag. • Cover with a hot, dry pan (see previous page) and leave the dough to rest for about 1 hour. • In the meantime pour very hot water over the bananas and raisins in a sieve and pat thoroughly dry. • Dice the bananas finely, mix with the raisins, rum or cognac and let them marinade, covered, while the filling is prepared. • Beat about half the butter with the honey, egg and egg yolk until very creamy, and flavor with the lemon rind, the vanilla and the cinnamon. • Gradually add the ricotta and cream, and beat everything until the mixture is light and airy. • Finally, mix in the candied lemon peel and the swollen fruit with the alcohol. • Preheat the oven to 350°F-400°F, and grease a baking tray with some of the remaining butter. • Cover the work surface with a large cloth and dust with some flour. • Roll out the strudel pastry as thinly as possible on the cloth, then run floured hands under it and pull out the pastry on all sides, until it is almost transparent. • Cut off any remaining thick edges which you cannot pull out any more with scissors or a knife. • Melt a scant half of the remaining butter and brush the pastry with it. • Mix the graham cracker crumbs with the sieved-off bran and sprinkle on the pastry, leaving a 1 in. border. • Spread the filling smoothly onto the pastry and fold over the pastry border on the short sides. Roll up the pastry with the help of the cloth from a long side and press the edges well down onto the roll. Now let the strudel roll straight onto the baking tray from the cloth, so that the pastry edges are underneath. • Melt the butter that you still have left and brush the strudel all over with it. • Place the baking tray on the middle shelf of the hot oven and bake the strudel for 45-55 minutes. • After about 35 minutes spread the cream little by little on the top of the strudel, and allow it to bake golden brown. • Take the strudel out of the oven and serve immediately, or else while it is still warm.

Yellow Plum Flan with Marzipan

Cut into 12 pieces

345 calories per serving
Preparation time: about 1½ hours
Cooling time: about 1½ hours
Baking time: 35-45 minutes

For the pastry:
1¾ cups wholewheat flour, freshly ground
½ cup millet meal
½ cup sour cream
2 tbs. honey
Pinch salt
½ tsp. vanilla extract
½ cup chilled butter
Butter for greasing
Graham cracker crumbs for sprinkling
For filling and decoration:
1⅓ cups almonds
3¼ cups yellow plums
1 cup honey
1-2 tbs. yellow plum liqueur
3 egg whites
Pinch salt

For the pastry knead all the ingredients quickly until smooth, shape into a ball and cool for 1 hour, wrapped in plastic wrap. • Preheat the oven to 400°F-425°F. Grease an 11 in. diameter spring-release pan and sprinkle with crumbs. • Press the pastry into this, making a rim ½ in. high, and prick the base several times with a fork. Bake for 20-25 minutes on the middle shelf of the hot oven, then allow to cool a little. • In the meantime, soak the almonds in boiling water, cool down, skin, and dry thoroughly. • Wash, dry and pit the yellow plums. • Grind about ½ cup almonds very finely in the blender or food-processor, adding ½ cup honey and the liqueur. Chop the rest of the almonds finely. • Beat the egg-whites with the sale until stiff enough to show the cut of a knife, and fold in the remaining honey. • Turn up the oven to 425°F-450°F, using heat from the top of the oven if possible. Mix a good half of the egg-white snow with the marzipan, spread over the flan, and lay the plums on top. • Put the rest of the snow into a piping-bag with a star-shaped nozzle, and pipe a lattice onto the flan. Sprinkle this with the chopped almonds and bake very hot for 15-20 minutes on the middle shelf, until it goes light brown. Slide the flan onto a wire rack and allow to cool. Serve fresh.

Gooseberry Cake with Barley and Hazelnuts

Cut into 12 pieces

405 calories per serving
Time for soaking and oven-drying: 11-13 hours
Preparation time: about 1 hour
Cooling time: about 30 minutes
Baking time: 45-50 minutes

1 cup whole barley grains
1 cup water for soaking
1½ cups hazelnuts
1½ cups wholewheat flour, freshly ground
1½ cups millet meal
Pinch salt
1 egg
5 tbs. honey
½ tsp. ground cinnamon
½ cup chilled butter
3¼ cups gooseberries
Wheatflour for rolling out
3 eggs, separated
1 cup heavy cream

Put the barley grains in 2¼ cups water to soak for 10-12 hours. • Drain the barley at the end of this time, but do not dry. • Preheat the oven to 160°F. • Spread out the barley on a baking tray and dry in the oven for about 1 hour, turning occasionally. Allow them to roast lightly, too, and put on a plate to cool. • While the barley is drying, grind about ⅓ cup hazelnuts and chop the rest finely. • For the pastry, mix the wheatflour with 1 cup millet and the ground hazelnuts and put on the work surface. Make a well in the center and put in the salt, egg, 1 tablespoon honey and ¼ teaspoon ground cinnamon. • Cut the chilled butter into very small pieces, and dot around the edge. Chop all the ingredients to a crumb texture, knead quickly to a smooth dough, shape into a ball and place in the refrigerator for about 30 minutes, wrapped in a plastic bag or plastic wrap. • Wash the gooseberries in cold water, pat dry and top and tail with scissors. Then prick the gooseberries several times with a needle or fine wooden skewer, so that they do not explode too much during cooking. • Preheat the oven to 400°F. • Dust the work surface lightly with flour and roll out the pastry thinly. Line an 11 in. diameter spring-release pan with it, making a rim 1-1½. high, and prick the base several times with a fork. • Beat the egg yolks with the remaining honey and cinnamon until creamy-white. • Whip both the cream and egg-whites until stiff, and slide them onto the egg-yolk mixture. Sieve the remaining millet flour over this and fold everything lightly but carefully together. • Finally, stir in the dried barley, the gooseberries and the chopped hazelnuts. • Fill the prepared pan with the mixture, smooth the surface, and bake for 45-50 minutes on the lower shelf of the preheated oven, until the mixture is well-cooked and the filling is firm. • If the top should brown too much during baking, cover with wax paper or aluminum foil. • Allow the cake to steam off for a short while in the pan, then place on a wire rack to cool and serve as fresh as possible, so that the gooseberries do not exude too much juice.

Cookies and Candies

It simply doesn't follow that people who are conscious of good nutrition do not "nibble" at sweet things. Why shouldn't they? After all, it depends entirely on what is eaten. In this chapter I have put together recipes for cookies and fancy small cakes, which are all prepared with freshly ground grain and without refined sugar. Sweetness is added with honey, syrup or dried fruit, and flavor added with nuts, seeds and spices. You can choose between Nut and Almond Cookies, Spicy Slices and Almond Meringue Pyramids, or if your appetite is a bit larger, Ricotta and Apple Pasties with Brazil nuts, and Wheat Dumplings with Mozzarella filling. Then there's something Christmassy with Cinnamon Stars, Honey Brezels and Spekulatius. Children will be delighted with Granola Bars and Oat and Nut Caramels, adults with Florentine Almond Cookies, Hazelnut Truffles with cherries in brandy, and Butter Truffles with apricot or marzipan.

Ricotta and Apple Pastries with Brazil Nuts

12 pieces

410 calories per serving
Preparation time (including cooling time): about 1 hour
Baking time: about 25 minutes

For the pastry:

1¾ cups wholewheat flour, freshly ground
1 cup linseeds, finely ground
Pinch salt
½ tsp. ground cinnamon
½ tsp. baking-powder
1¾ cups ricotta cheese
1 egg
1 cup chilled butter
In addition:
2 tbs. butter
1 cup oat flakes
½ cup raisins
2 tbs. rum
2¼ cups cooking apples
Juice of 1 lemon
Wheatflour for rolling out
½ cup Brazil nuts, finely chopped
5 tbs. honey
1 egg yolk
2 tbs. heavy cream
Butter for greasing

For the pastry, mix the wheat and linseed flours with the salt, ground cinnamon and baking-powder, and pile onto the work surface. Make a well in the center, put in the ricotta (drained) and the egg, and distribute the butter in very small pieces around the flour. • Chop all the ingredients with two knives until they are mixed together with a coarse crumb texture, then knead them very quickly to a smooth dough with cooled hands. • Shape into a ball, and place in the refrigerator, wrapped in plastic wrap, until the filling is ready. • For this, melt the butter gently in a pan and roast the oat flakes in it until golden brown, stirring constantly. Leave to cool on a plate. • Wash the raisins briefly in a sieve under hot water, and rub well dry in a cloth. Then put them in a bowl with the rum, and allow to soak, covered, for a few minutes. • In the meantime, peel, quarter and core the apples, and grate coarsely. Mix immediately with the lemon juice, so that the apple does not go brown. • Preheat the oven to 425°F. • Roll out the pastry on a lightly floured surface to just ¼ in. thick, and cut into 4 in. squares. • Mix the grated apple with the rum-and-raisins, the Brazil nuts, and about ½ cup roasted oatflakes, and pile into the middle of the pastry squares.

Dribble 3 tablespoons honey over them. • Whisk the egg yolk with the cream and use part of this to brush the edges of the pastry. • Fold the squares diagonally, pressing the edges well together. • Lay the pastries on a greased baking-tray and brush the tops with the remaining egg. Put on the middle shelf of the hot oven. • Bake the apple pastries for about 20 minutes, then brush the tops with the remaining honey, warmed. Sprinkle with the remaining oat-flakes. • Allow this glaze to caramelize for another 3-4 minutes in the oven, and then place the pastries on a wire rack to cool. They should be served as fresh as possible, as the pastry easily becomes tough if it is left to stand.

Marzipan Slices with Sesame

Cut into 35 pieces

135 calories per serving
Preparation time: about 1 hour
Cooling time: about 45 minutes
Baking time: 20-25 minutes

1 cup almonds
½ cup honey
1 cup butter
Pinch vanilla extract
2¼ cups wholewheat flour, freshly ground
½ cup buckwheat flour, freshly ground
1 cup sesame seeds
Wheatflour for rolling out
3 tbs. honey
2 tsp. lemon juice

Scald the almonds with boiling water and leave to soak in it for 1-2 minutes. Then cool down with cold water and immediately push the brown skins off the nuts with your fingertips. Dry the almonds very well on a cloth. • Afterwards grind the almonds as finely as possible in a blender or food-processor, gradually adding the honey. Continue to mix them until a smooth marzipan is formed. • Cut the butter into small flakes, add to the marzipan with the vanilla and stir together until creamy. • Mix the wholewheat flour with the ground buckwheat on the work surface, add the butter and marzipan mixture and knead everything very quickly to a smooth dough. • Shape this into a ball, and place in the refrigerator for 45 minutes, wrapped in plastic wrap. • In the meantime roast the sesame seeds in a dry pan until golden-brown, stirring them constantly, and cool off on a plate. • Preheat the oven to 350°F. • Roll out the pastry on a lightly floured surface to about ¾ in. thick, and cut into slices 3 in. long by 1½ in. wide. Lay them on an ungreased baking tray, and bake until light brown on the middle shelf of the oven. •

Meanwhile, warm the honey with the lemon juice. • Remove the slices from the tray, brush thinly with the honey mixture, and sprinkle with sesame seeds. Then leave to cool.

Nut Pretzels

Made into 10 pieces

260 calories serving
Preparation time: about 1 hour
Cooling time: about 45 minutes
Baking time: about 15 minutes

1¾ cups wholewheat flour, freshly ground
½ cup buckwheat flour, finely ground
½ cup soft butter
3 tbs. honey
Pinch salt
Grated rind of ½ lemon
1 egg
½ cup skinned almonds, finely ground
½ cup pistachios, very finely chopped
Wheatflour for shaping
1 tbs. lemon juice
1 tbs. white rum

Mix the two flours together. • Cream the butter with 2 tablespoon honey, adding the

salt, grated lemon rind and the egg. When everything is well combined, work in the flour and then divide the mixture into 2 halves. • Knead the almonds into one half of the pastry and the pistachios into the other, and shape both into balls. Wrap these in plastic wrap and leave to rest in the refrigerator for about 45 minutes. • Preheat the oven to 350°F. • Take the pastry out of the refrigerator one portion at a time, flour the work surface lightly, and shape into rolls about 12 in. long and at least as thick as a pencil. Twist into pretzel shapes, pressing the ends down firmly. • Lay the pretzels on an ungreased baking tray, and bake on the middle shelf of the hot oven until light brown . • Meanwhile, warm the remaining honey with the lemon juice and the rum, ready for glazing. • When the pretzels are cooked,

place them on a wire rack and brush with the glaze, then allow to cool.

Nut Triangles

20 pieces

225 calories per serving
Preparation time: about 45 minutes
Cooling time: about 30 minutes
Baking time: 20-25 minutes

For the pastry:
1½ cups wholewheat flour, freshly ground
½ cup linseeds, roughly ground
½ cup hazelnuts, finely ground
1 egg
Pinch salt
3 tbs. honey
½ cup chilled butter
4 tbs. heavy cream
For the top and decoration:
¾ cup butter

1¼ cups honey
2 cups hazelnuts, flaked
½ cup sesame seeds
3 tbs. maple syrup
1 tsp. carob powder

Mix the wheatflour with the linseed and the hazelnuts and make a well in the center. Put into this the egg with the salt and honey, and place the butter, in very small pieces, around the flour at the edge. • Chop all the ingredients to a crumb texture with two knives, then knead to a smooth dough from the outside in. • Wrap in plastic wrap and leave to rest in the refrigerator for 30 minutes. • Preheat the oven to 400°F. • Roll out the pastry onto an ungreased baking tray and spread the cream over it. • Heat ½ cup butter and the honey in a saucepan, stirring until they have blended together. Stir in the hazelnuts and sesame

seeds and allow to cool slightly. • Spread this mixture onto the pastry and bake for 20-25 minutes on the middle shelf of the hot oven until golden brown. • While still hot, cut into squares and then cut these diagonally into triangles. Cool on a wire rack. • Cook the remaining butter with the maple syrup and the carob powder, stirring well, until it thickens. Spread on the corners of the cookies while still hot.

Oat Cookies with Dates and Ginger

Makes 18 pieces

340 calories per serving
Preparation time: about 1 hour
Baking time: about 20 minutes

2½ cups dried dates
4 pieces whole stem ginger in syrup

1⅓ cup soft butter

Pinch salt

1 tsp. ground ginger

1 tsp. ground cinnamon

1¼ cups pear juice concentrate

Grated rind of 1½ oranges and 1 lemon

4 tbs. pear liqueur

2½ cups wholewheat flour, freshly ground

3½ cups jumbo oatflakes

Butter for greasing

S tone the dates, drain the stem ginger and dice both very finely. • Cream the butter with the salt, ground ginger and cinnamon in a bowl with the pear juice concentrate, adding the grated orange and lemon rind and the pear liqueur. • Preheat the oven to 400°F. • Mix the wheatflour with the oat flakes, and the date and ginger pieces and add to the bowl,

ready to make the pastry. Only mix the ingredients together lightly, so that they are evenly mixed, but still loose. • Grease a baking tray with butter and spread about two-thirds of the pastry smoothly onto it. • Crumble the rest of the pastry mixture over it with your fingertips, and bake until golden brown on the middle shelf of the hot oven. • After cooling, cut the slab of cookie into slices about 2 × 4 in., and place on a wire rack to cool further.

Fruity Diamonds

Makes 40 pieces

115 calories per serving
Soaking time: about 30 minutes
Preparation time: about 40 minutes
Cooling time: about 30 minutes
Baking time: about 15 minutes

1 cup mixed dried fruit

3 tbs. cognac or rum

2 tbs. almond liqueur

1¾ cups wholewheat flour, freshly ground

½ tsp. baking powder

1¾ cups tender whole rolled oats with bran

½ cup linseeds

¼ cup sesame seeds

½ cup cashew nuts, coarsely chopped

¾ cup butter

½ cup honey

2 eggs

Wheatflour for rolling out

Butter for greasing

2 tbs. heavy cream

1 egg yolk for brushing

W ash the dried fruit briefly in hot water and rub thoroughly dry. Then dice the fruit, pour over the cognac or rum

and the almond liqueur and leave to soak, covered, for about 30 minutes. • Mix the wheatflour on the work surface with the baking powder, oatflakes, linseeds, sesame seeds and cashew nuts, and make a well in the center. Cream the butter with the honey and eggs and put into the well with the fruit and alcohol. • Knead all the ingredients quickly together, shape into a ball, and allow to rest in the refrigerator, wrapped in plastic wrap, for about 30 minutes. • Preheat the oven to 425°F. On a lightly floured surface, roll out the pastry about ¼ in. thick, cut into diamonds with 2-2½ in. sides, and brush with the cream and egg yolk, whisked together. • Bake the diamonds for about 15 minutes on a greased baking tray on the middle shelf of the oven. • Cool on a wire rack.

Three Grain Waffles with Almonds

Makes 7

450 calories per serving
Preparation time: about 1 hour
Soaking time: 30 minutes

¾ cup butter
3 eggs, separated
½ cup honey
2 pinches vanilla extract
2 tbs. cream
1 cup wholewheat flour, freshly ground
½ cup linseeds
1 tsp. baking powder
Pinch salt
½ cup sesame seeds
½ cup almonds, very finely chopped or freshly ground
Butter for greasing

Cream the butter well, gradually adding the egg yolks, honey, vanilla and the cream. • Mix the wheatflour with the linseeds and the baking powder. Stir into the butter mixture and allow to rest for about 30 minutes, so that the wheat and linseeds can swell. • Whisk the egg whites with the salt to a snow that will hold the cut of a knife. Slide it on top of the mixture, and then fold in together with the sesame seeds and almonds. • Heat the waffle-iron according to the instructions and grease it. Put in some mixture, smooth it lightly and close the iron. • Cook the waffles for about 4-6 minutes (depending on your equipment) until they are light brown on both sides, and lay them next to each other on a wire rack to cool.

Variations: Walnut Waffles with Pears. • Prepare the mixture as described above, and mix in an additional 1 tablespoon wheatflour. Wash 3 pears and core them. Grate 2 of them into strips and cut the remaining one into slices. Pour lemon juice over them immediately. Replace the almonds with finely chopped

walnuts, and fold into the flour together with the grated pear, sesame and egg white snow. Bake and cool the waffles, and decorate with pear slices.

Old Fashioned Girdle Cakes

Makes 8

245 calories per serving
Preparation time: about 1 hour
Soaking time: about 20 minutes
Baking time: 4-6 minutes

½ cup butter
3 tbs. honey
3 eggs, separated
1¼ cups ricotta cheese
Grated rind of ½ lemon
½ tsp. cinnamon powder
1 cup wholewheat flour, freshly ground
½ cup millet, finely ground
½ cup seltzer or soda water
Pinch salt
Butter for greasing

Cream the butter until light and fluffy, gradually adding the honey, egg yolks and ricotta cheese. Flavor with the grated lemon rind and the cinnamon. • Mix the wheatflour with the ground millet, and stir into the butter carefully, alternating with the mineral water. • Leave to rest for 20 minutes so that the flour can soak. • Whisk the egg whites with the salt until they are stiff enough to hold the cut of a knife. Wait until just before baking to fold gently into the mixture. • Heat the waffle iron according to instructions and grease, put in some mixture and, with the iron closed, allow to become light brown. This takes 4-6 minutes, according to your equipment. • Put the waffles immediately onto a wire rack to

cool. • Bake waffles in the same way with the rest of the mixture. To cool, always place them beside each other on the rack, so that they do not go soft and stick together. Serve them fresh, as soon as possible after cooling.

Hazelnut Waffles with Chocolate and Cream

Makes 8

570 calories per serving
Preparation time: about 1½ hours
Soaking time: about 15 minutes

¾ cup soft butter
3 tbs. honey
4 eggs
Pinch salt
1½ cups wholewheat flour, freshly ground
½ cup millet, finely ground
1 tsp. baking powder
1-2 tsp. carob powder
7 oz. cartons heavy cream
1 cup hazelnuts, freshly ground
½ tsp. vanilla extract
4 oz. milk chocolate
Butter for greasing

Cream the butter until light and fluffy, gradually adding the honey, eggs and salt. • Mix the wheatflour with the ground millet, the baking powder and the carob and stir into the mixture with 5-6 tablespoons of cream. Finally mix in the hazelnuts and the vanilla. • Leave the dough to rest for about 15 minutes, so that the flour can soak. • In the meantime, grate the chocolate coarsely. Whip the remaining cream until stiff, put in a bowl and place, covered, in the refrigerator. • Heat the waffle iron

according to the instructions and grease. • Put some mixture in the iron, remove the excess, and close the iron. Bake the waffles for 4-6 minutes (according to your equipment), and cool on a wire rack. • Make waffles in the same way with the remaining mixture, and allow to cool. Decorate them with a blob of cream, and sprinkle with the chocolate.

Spicy Slices with Dried Fruit

Makes 30

190 calories per serving
Preparation time: about 45 minutes
Resting time: 2-3 hours
Baking time: 20-25 minutes

For the dough:
⅔ cup figs
⅔ cup dates, pitted

¼ cup candied orange peel
¼ cup candied lemon peel
2 glasses (each 1 oz.) cognac or rum
2¾ cups sugar-beet syrup
½ cup butter
1¾ cups wholewheat flour, freshly ground
½ cups millet, finely ground
½ cups buckwheat, finely ground
3 tsp. baking powder
1 tsp. ground cinnamon
2 pinches ground allspice
2 pinches nutmeg, freshly grated
Pinch salt
Pinch each ground aniseed and coriander
1¼ cups hazelnuts, chopped
Wheatflour for rolling out

For decoration:
1 cup almonds
2 tbs. sugar-beet syrup
2 tbs. cognac or rum

Rinse off the figs and dates with hot water, pat dry and dice finely. Cut the candied peel similarly into small cubes and put into a small bowl with the dates and figs. Pour over the cognac or rum, stir, and allow everything to marinade, covered, until the other ingredients are ready. • Gently warm the sugar-beet syrup and the butter, stirring together, but do not let them get hot. Cool down again to hand temperature, or cooler, in a bowl. • Using a large bowl, mix the wheat, millet and buckwheat flours with the baking powder, cinnamon, allspice, nutmeg and salt, as well as the aniseed and coriander. Make a well in the center. • Pour in the butter and syrup, and add the softened dried fruit, including any alcohol which has not been absorbed, and the hazelnuts. Work everything well together, working first

from the middle outwards, then kneading in the flour left at the sides, until all the ingredients hold together well. • Now wrap the dough in plastic wrap, or cover the bowl well, and place in the refrigerator for 2-3 hours. • During this time, scald the almonds with boiling water, cool them down quickly with cold water, and push off the skins. • Cut the almonds in half lengthways and rub well dry on a tea-towel. • Preheat the oven to 350°F-400°F. • Work the dough over once more and, using a surface dusted with flour, roll out to about ¼ in. thick. Cut it into rectangles 2-2½ in. with a pastry wheel or a sharp knife. Then place them on a baking tray lined with wax paper. • Warm the sugar-beet syrup with the cognac or rum over a low heat, until they are mixed. • Brush the rectangles with it and lay the al-

mond halves on them. Place the baking tray on the middle shelf of the hot oven, and bake the slices for 20-25 minutes. • Remove from the paper and allow to cool.

Meringue and Almond Pyramids

Makes 30

65 calories
Preparation time: about 1 hour
Baking time: 40-45 minutes

1⅔ cups almonds
3 tsp. soy flour
3 tbs. cold water
2 very fresh egg whites
Pinch salt
1 cup honey
½ tsp. lemon juice
½ tsp. vanilla extract

Scald the almonds with boiling water, leaving them in there for a few seconds, then cool them down with cold water and remove the brown skins. Dry them thoroughly on a cloth, and then chop them finely. • Put the soy flour in a small bowl and stir it well with the water. • Whisk the egg whites in a bowl with the salt until it is stiff. Add the honey and the soy mixture, continuing to beat it in constantly and vigorously. • Continue working, until the mixture is firm and very shiny. • Fold in gently the lemon juice and the vanilla, together with the chopped almonds. • Preheat the oven to 212°F-248°F. • Line a baking tray with wax paper, and place little pyramids on it using two teaspoons. Place them on the middle shelf of the oven and let them dry out rather than bake. Do not let them become too brown. You can prop the oven door open a little with the handle of a wooden spoon, so that the moisture can escape. • Remove the Meringue and Almond Pyramids immediately from the paper using a palette knife, and allow them to dry off further and cool down on a wire rack.

Vanilla Crescents with Chocolate Tips

Makes 45

85 calories per serving
Preparation time: about 45 minutes
Cooling time: about 1 hour
Baking time: 10-15 minutes

1½ cups wholewheat flour, freshly ground
1½ cups millet flour
1 cup almonds, freshly grated
1 egg yolk
Pinch salt
2 tbs. honey
1 tsp. vanilla extract
¾ cup chilled butter
4 oz. milk chocolate

Sieve the wheatflour, put the bran on one side and then mix the flour on a work surface with the millet flour and the almonds. • Make a well in the center, and put into it the egg yolk, salt, honey and vanilla extract. Cut the butter into small flakes and dot over the flour. • Using two knives, chop all the ingredients to a crumb texture, and knead very quickly to a smooth dough with your hands well cooled (Rinse them under a cold tap and dry). • Make this dough into a roll about 2 in. in diameter and place, covered, in the refrigerator for at least 1 hour. • Preheat the oven to 350°F and sprinkle the work surface with

the bran. • Cut ½ in. thick slices from the roll and shape them on the work surface to crescents, about 2½ in. long and ½ in. thick, with pointed ends. • Shape into half-moons and place on an ungreased baking tray. Place them immediately on the middle shelf of the hot oven, and bake until golden brown. Cool on a wire rack. • Melt the chocolate in a double boiler over low heat, and allow it to cool a little. • Dip both ends of the crescents into the chocolate, and allow this glaze to harden.

Hearts with Flaked Almonds

Makes 30

55 calories per serving
Preparation time: about 1 hour
Cooling time: 2-3 hours
Baking time: 15-20 minutes

| 1¾ cups wholewheat flour, freshly ground |
| 1 cup millet, flour |
| 5 tbs. sour cream |
| 4 tbs. honey |
| ½ tsp. vanilla extract |
| Butter for greasing |
| Wheatflour for rolling out |
| ½ cup almonds, flaked |

Mix the wheat and millet flours and make a well in the center. Into it put the sour cream with 1 tablespoon honey and the vanilla, and knead everything very quickly to a smooth dough. • Shape the dough into a ball and place in the refrigerator for 2-3 hours, wrapped in plastic wrap. • Grease a baking tray, heat the oven to 350°F-400°F and dust the work surface lightly with flour. • Roll out the pastry in portions to about ¼ in. thick, and press out heart shapes with sides about 2½ in. long. • Warm the remaining honey until it is thin and runny, and use it to brush the heart-shapes. Sprinkle on the flaked almonds and bake on the middle shelf of the hot oven. Bake for 15-20 minutes until light brown. • Remove from the tray and cool on a wire rack.

Almond Fancies

Makes 50

115 calories per serving
reparation time: about 1 hour
Cooling time: about 2 hours
Baking time: about 15 minutes

| ¼ lb. almonds |
| 2 cups honey |
| 1 tsp. rose water |
| 1 tbs. almond liqueur |
| 1¼ cups soft butter |
| Pinch salt |
| 2 tsp. cinnamon powder |

| 2 pinches ground cloves |
| 1 tsp. vanilla extract |
| Grated rind of ½ lemon |
| 1 egg |
| 3 cups wholewheat flour, freshly ground |
| 1½ cups millet flour |
| Butter for greasing |
| ⅔ cup almonds, flaked |
| Wheatflour for dusting |
| 2-3 tbs. milk |

Scald the almonds with boiling water, skin and dry thoroughly on a cloth. • Then grind as finely as possible in a blender, gradually adding the honey, rose water and almond liqueur, and work everything to a smooth marzipan. • Cream the butter with the salt, spice, vanilla, lemon rind and egg until light and fluffy, and then work gradually into the marzipan mixture. •

Mix the wheat and millet flour and stir part of it into the mixture, but knead in the rest. • Shape the dough into a ball, wrap in plastic wrap and cool for 2 hours. • Grease a baking tray. • Preheat the oven to 400°F. • Sprinkle the work surface with the flaked almonds. • Dust a selection of small fancy cookie cutters very lightly with flour, then press in some dough and level off the surface with a thin wire, or a knife with a very fine blade. • Now place cookie cutters on the surface in such a way that they rest with the underside on the flaked almonds. Press these on lightly and place the cookies on the baking tray. • Brush the tops with milk and bake the cookies on the middle shelf of the hot oven for about 15 minutes, until golden brown. Cool on a wire rack.

Cinnamon Stars

Makes 40

120 calories per serving
Preparation time: about 1 hour
Baking time: 30-45 minutes

4 cups almonds
2 cups honey
1 tsp. rose water
2 tsp. cinnamon powder
5 egg whites
Pinch salt
1 tsp. lemon juice
3-4 tbs. wheat bran for rolling out
Butter for greasing

Scald almonds with boiling water, skin and dry thoroughly on a cloth. • Then grind the almonds as finely as possible in the blender or food processor, adding 1¼ cups honey, the rose water and the cinnamon, and

work everything to a smooth marzipan. • Put the remaining almonds through a nut mill with their skins intact. • Whisk the egg whites with the salt until stiff. • Carry on whisking and gradually add the remaining honey and the lemon juice. • Leave about 5 tablespoons of this mixture to one side. • Stir the remaining egg white snow into the marzipan with a spoon, and mix in carefully the ground almonds. At the end the dough should be very firm. • Preheat the oven to 300°F. • Lay a piece of wax paper on a baking tray and grease with butter. • Dust the work surface with bran and roll out the pastry on it, in portions, to about ¼ in. thick. • Cut out stars about 2 in. in diameter and place on the tray. • Spread the remaining egg white snow on the stars and place the baking tray on the middle shelf of the preheated oven. •

Let the Cinnamon Stars dry out rather than cook, for 30-45 minutes, without letting them brown too much.

Honey Cake Pretzels

Makes 30

80 calories per serving
Preparation time: about 1½ hours
Resting time: 12-24 hours
Baking time: about 20 minutes

2½ cups honey
¼ cup water
1¾ cups wholewheat flour, freshly ground
½ cup rye flour
2 pinches ground mixed spice
1 tsp. baking powder
2 tbs. lemon peel
2 tbs. candied orange peel
½ cup almonds, peeled and halved

⅓ cup dried figs
3 red and 3 green candied cherries
1 cup almonds, peeled and flaked
Pinch salt
½ tsp. vanilla extract
½ cup millet flour
½ cup sesame seeds
¼ cup butter
⅓ cup milk
½ cup heavy cream
1 cup honey
6 oz. milk chocolate

Finely dice the candied peel, dates and figs, cut the cherries into tiny slices and crumble the almonds lightly. Mix everything with the salt, vanilla, millet flour and sesame seeds. • Bring to a boil the butter, milk, cream and honey, put in the fruit and almond mixture and simmer for about 5 minutes, stirring continuously. • Preheat the oven to 350°F. • Place the mixture in a double boiler. • Lay a sheet of wax paper on a baking tray. • Using a tablespoon, make small heaps of almond mixture on the paper and then use a damp knife to spread them into thin cookies about 2½ in. in diameter. • Bake for about 20 minutes on the middle shelf of the hot oven, and then remove immediately and cool on a wire rack. • Melt the chocolate in a double boiler. • As soon as it begins to set again, spread thickly on the undersides of the biscuits. • Allow this layer to dry a little, then with a fork or serrated knife make wavy lines, and leave to set.

Pineapple Granola

Makes 36

160 calories per serving
Time for soaking and drying out: 12-13 hours
Preparation time: about 45 minutes
Baking time: about 30 minutes

¼ cup whole wheat berries

Butter for greasing
Wheatflour for rolling out
2 tbs. rum

Warm 2¼ cups honey with the water over a low heat, until they are mixed together. • Mix the wheat and rye flour with the spice and baking powder. • Dice the candied orange and lemon peel very finely. • Add the honey mixture to the flour, put in the candied peel and work everything to a smooth dough, first stirring with a wooden spoon,

then kneading. • Allow the dough to rest, covered, overnight. • Grease a baking tray and preheat the oven to 400°F. • Knead the dough again on a floured surface, and roll out to just ¼ in. thick. Cut into strips ¼ in. wide and 6 in. long. Make these into rolls and twist into pretzel shapes. • Warm the remaining honey gently with the rum, brush the pretzels with it and decorate each one with two almond halves. • Bake the pretzels for about 20 minutes on the

baking tray on the middle shelf of the hot oven, then allow to cool.

Florentines

Makes 35

105 calories per serving
Preparation time: about 45 minutes
Baking time: about 20 minutes

2 tbs. candied lemon peel
2 tbs. candied orange peel
⅓ cup dried dates, pitted

water
1¼ cups dried pineapple
2½ cups cashew nuts
1¼ cups sesame seeds
1 cup whole oat flakes
½ cup butter
1 cup honey
1 cup heavy cream
Pinch salt
½ tsp. ground ginger
Grated rind of ½ lemon
Oil for brushing

The wheat berries need about 2½ times their volume of water for soaking. Use a measuring jug for the berries that you can also use to measure the water. • Pour the water over the wheat berries and allow to soak for 11-12 hours. • Then drain the berries and preheat the oven to 160°F. • Spread the berries out loosely on a baking tray and

dry out in the oven for about 1 hour, turning frequently. • Cut the dried pineapple into small pieces. • Chop the cashew nuts coarsely and mix into the pieces of pineapple with the sesame seeds and the oat flakes. • Cut the butter into small flakes and put into a wide saucepan. Add the honey and cream, together with the salt, ground ginger and grated lemon rind and, stirring well, let it come to a boil. • Mix in the pineapple mixture together with the soaked, dried, wheat, and let it simmer for 3 minutes, stirring, until the mixture begins to thicken. • Preheat the oven to 400°F. • Lay a sheet of aluminum foil on a baking tray—if it has an open edge, fold the foil several times to form a smooth border. • Brush the foil with oil and spread the Granola Bar mixture on it smoothly with a lightly oiled or damp knife. • Place the

baking tray on the middle shelf of the hot oven and allow the mixture to bake for about 30 minutes. • Take the tray out of the oven and cut the mixture into bars about 1½ in. wide by 3 in. long, using an oiled knife. • Allow these to cool a little, break them completely apart and allow to cool on a wire rack. • Store, wrapped individually in cellophane or wax paper.

Variations:
Peach Granola Bars with Chocolate. • Soften ¼ cup wheat berries as given above and dry them in the oven. Finely dice 1¼ cups dried peaches and mix with 1⅔ cup peeled almonds, coarsely chopped, ½ cup whole oat flakes, ¼ cup finely ground rice, and ½ cup each of sesame seeds and sunflower seeds. • Bring to a boil in a saucepan ½ cup butter

with 1¼ cup honey and 1 cup heavy cream. Flavor with a pinch of salt, the scraped-out pulp of a vanilla pod and the grated rind of ½ orange. Put in the peach and almond mixture and the dried wheat, and bake in the prepared pan. Cut into bars while still hot and cool on a wire rack. When they are completely cool, melt 6 oz. milk chocolate in a double boiler. Dip the bars into it in such a way that the undersides and part of the edges are coated. Lay the bars on a wire rack to dry, chocolate side up.

Fritters with Sweet Mozzarella Filling

Makes 15

235 calories
Time for soaking, drying and proving: about 11 hours
Preparation time: about 1 hour

½ cup whole wheat berries

1 cup warm water

1¾ cup buckwheat, finely ground

¼ cup yeast

½ cup warm milk

2 tbs. sour cream

3 egg yolks

2 pinches salt

4 tbs. honey

1¾ cups wholewheat flour, freshly ground

½ cup pine nuts

1½ cups mozzarella cheese

⅓ cup each dried pineapple and figs

2 pinches cinnamon powder

Wheat or buckwheat flour for shaping

2¼ cups vegetable fat or melted butter for frying

Measure the volume of the wheat in a measuring jug.

Then place the wheat in a large bowl and pour over it 2½ times its volume of water (measured similarly in the jug), and allow the grains to soak for about 10 hours. • Then set the oven to 160°F and drain the wheat, but do not dry. • Spread out the grains on a baking tray and dry in the oven for 50-60 minutes, turning several times. • About 30 minutes before the end of the drying time, put the buckwheat flour in a bowl and make a well in the center. • Crumble in the yeast and work it into a dough in the well with some of the milk and a little flour from the sides. Cover the bowl with a cloth and allow the dough to rise in a warm, draft-free place, until bubbles appear. According to room temperature, this takes 15-20 minutes. • Add the remaining milk, together with the sour cream, egg yolks, salt and 2 ta-

blespoons honey. Work everything to a smooth dough and beat until it bubbles. Cover with a cloth again and allow to stand for at least 20 minutes. • In the meantime remove the wheat from the oven and allow to cool to hand temperature, turning frequently. • Knead the dough once more vigorously and mix in the wheat, kneading it in gradually. The dough must end up firm and no longer sticky, but not dry. • Now let the dough rest again for a few minutes while you prepare the filling. Chop the pine nuts coarsely and roast them in a dry frying pan until golden brown, stirring constantly. Allow to cool. • Drain the mozzarella and cut into small cubes. • Rinse the dried fruit under hot water, pat thoroughly dry and cut into small cubes. Mix everything into the cubes of mozzarella, together with the cinnamon and the re-

maining honey. • Dust the work surface with some flour. Shape the dough into a roll, cut into 15 pieces and either press them flat on the surface or roll them out into rounds. • Put a teaspoon of filling in the middle of each one and fold the dough over it. Using floured hands, roll them into small balls and lay them on a floured baking tray. • Heat the fat in a saucepan, not too large, to 350°F. Fry the dumplings in it until golden brown, about 1½ minutes. Cook them a few at a time, turning them, but do not let them touch each other, or they will stick together. • You must not let the fat cool down too much, otherwise the dumplings will not cook through quickly enough and will absorb too much fat. • Thoroughly remove the fat from the dumplings on paper towel and cool on a wire rack. • Serve fresh, and if you like, pour some honey over them.

Pan Doughnuts with Potato and Buckwheat

Makes 50

75 calories
Preparation time: about 30 minutes
Cooling time: 12-24 hours
Final preparation and cooking time: about 1 hour

3½ cups floury potatoes
1¾ cup ricotta cheese
2 egg yolks
Grated rind of ½ lemon
3 tbs. honey
1 tbs. rum
2 egg whites
Pinch salt
1¾ cups buckwheat flour, freshly ground
4 cups vegetable fat or clarified butter for frying
1-2 tsp. cinnamon powder

Scrub the potatoes thoroughly under cold running water, and cook in their skins. • Peel the potatoes and let them cool down overnight. • The next day, grate the potatoes. • Cream the ricotta with the egg yolks, grated lemon rind, honey and rum. • Stir the grated potato thoroughly into the ricotta mixture. • Whisk the egg whites with the salt until they are stiff and slide onto the ricotta mixture. • Sieve the buckwheat flour over it and fold everything together as gently as possible, to give a really firm dough. • Heat the vegetable fat or clarified butter in a deep fryer to 350°F. Immerse 2 tablespoons in it briefly, and use them to cut off little doughnuts from the dough. Before you cut off each doughnut immerse the spoons briefly in the fat again, so that they come away more easily. • When frying the doughnuts, make sure they go golden brown all over by turning them; lift them out with a draining spoon,

and place them on a thick layer of kitchen paper to absorb the fat. • Mix the grated coconut with the ground cinnamon and toss the doughnuts in it while they are still warm. • Allow to cool on a wire rack and serve fresh.

Oatflake and Nut Caramels

Makes 40

35 calories per serving
Preparation time: about 45 minutes
Cooling time: about 2 hours

½ cup hazelnuts, finely chopped
2 tbs. butter
½ cup honey
1 cup heavy cream
½ cup whole oat flakes
2 pinches cinnamon powder
Oil for brushing

Finely chopped hazelnuts and whole oat flakes for finishing off

Roast the hazelnuts in a dry pan until golden brown, stirring continuously, and remove from the heat, but do not let them cool completely. • In another pan, bring to a boil the butter, honey and cream and continue to boil, stirring until it thickens and becomes light brown in color. • Add the nuts, together with the oat flakes and cinnamon, and continue to boil and stir until the mixture is thick and sticky. • To test, let a drop of mixture fall into ice-cold water. If it hardens immediately, remove the pan from the heat. • Lay a sheet of aluminum foil on a baking tray, folding it high in the middle, or divide it with an oiled board. • Brush the foil with oil and spread the caramel mixture evenly over it. Sprinkle with

hazelnuts and oatflakes. • Allow the mixture to cool and set for about 1 hour, then brush the work surface with oil, turn it out and remove the foil. • Use an oiled knife to cut the caramels into 1 in. squares, or strips, and separate them. Leave in a cool place for a further hour. Wrap individually in cellophane, as they stick together easily. You must store them in a cool, dry place.

Sesame Candies with Pecans

Makes 30

55 calories per serving
Preparation time: about 30 minutes

¼ tbs. white gelatin
½ cup sesame seeds
½ cup pecans, finely chopped
2 tbs. butter

½ cup honey
Pinch saffron powder
1 tbs. water
1 tbs. rose water
1 tbs. rum
1 oz. pecan halves

Dissolve the gelatin in cold water according to the directions on the packet, and leave to soak. • Roast the sesame seeds and pecans lightly in a dry pan, stirring, and remove from heat. • Heat and stir the butter with the honey in another pan, until it becomes light brown. • Stir in the sesame and nut mixture and bring to a boil again. • Dissolve the saffron in the water and mix with the nut mixture together, the rose water and the rum. • Add the gelatin to the mixture. • Put the mixture into small paper cases, and stand in a cool place for a few minutes until

it shows signs of setting. • Place a pecan half on each candy and leave to set completely.

Pistachio Marzipan Balls

Makes 30

65 calories per serving
Preparation time: about 1 hour
Cooling time: about 30 minutes

1½ cups pistachios, shelled

1 cup light honey

Grated rind of ¼ lemon

1 tbs. rose water

2 drops bitter almond extract

1 cup pistachios, very finely chopped

Chop the pistachios and then grind in the food processor to a very fine, smooth purée. Leave the processor switched on while you gradually pour in the

honey, and continue to mix everything together until creamy. • Finally add the grated lemon rind, together with the rose water and bitter almond extract, and work in very thoroughly. • Leave the marzipan in a cool place for about 30 minutes, then shape them on the work surface into balls about the size of a walnut. • Put the finely chopped pistachios on a plate and roll the balls in them. Press this layer in lightly, put the Marzipan Balls into small paper cases and keep cool until required.

Variation: Almond Marzipan Bites. Prepare the marzipan using shelled and peeled almonds instead of pistachios and shape it into ovals, about the size of an almond and lightly pointed at one end. For decoration, press a peeled almond (roasted golden

brown if you like) onto each candy.

Apricot and Marzipan Rolls

Makes 15

135 calories per serving
Preparation time: about 1¼ hours

⅔ cup almonds

2 tbs. light honey

1 cup dried apricots

1 cup almonds, very finely chopped

Scald the almonds with boiling water and soak them for 1-2 minutes, then cool down quickly and remove the brown skins. • Dry them thoroughly on a cloth or thick layer of paper towel. Chop coarsely and reduce to a fine purée in the food pro-

cessor, gradually adding the honey. • Wash the apricots in hot water, dry, chop very finely and knead into the marzipan mixture. • Using a cold work surface, or even better a marble slab, shape the apricot marzipan into rolls 4 cm long and about as thick as your thumb; place them next to each other in the refrigerator. • Roast the finely chopped almonds in a dry pan, stirring, until golden brown, and put on a plate. • Roll the Apricot and Marzipan Rolls in the almonds while they are still slightly warm, press them lightly all around and return to a cool place until required. • To prevent them sticking together, the candies may be put in paper cases or wrapped in cellophane.

Hazelnut Balls with Cherries in Brandy

Makes 20

110 calories per serving
Preparation time: about 45
minutes
Cooling time: about 3 hours

1²⁄₃ cups hazelnuts
3 tbs honey
½ tsp vanilla extract
1 tbs nut liqueur
1 egg yolk
1–2 tbs cognac
20 cherries preserved in cognac
2 oz milk chocolate

Preheat the oven to 400°F. •
Spread out the hazelnuts on
a baking tray and roast for
10–15 minutes on the middle
shelf. • Shake the nuts into a
cloth and use it to rub off the
brown skins. • Let the nuts cool

off, then grind 1 cup of them as
finely as possible in the blender
or food processor. • During the
grinding, gradually add the
honey, vanilla and nut liqueur
and work everything to a smooth
marzipan. • Grate the rest of the
nuts with a nut mill and put into
a bowl. • Crumble the marzipan
into the nuts, also putting in the
egg yolk and cognac or brandy,
and work everything to a firm
mixture. • Cover the bowl and
place in the refrigerator for about
2 hours. • In the meantime, thoroughly drain the cherries and
grate the chocolate coarsely. •
Divide the nut mixture into 20
small portions and shape into
small flat circles. Put a cherry
into the middle of each one and
close the nut mixture around it,
pressing the edges carefully together. • Put the chocolate on a
plate, toss the filled Hazelnut
Balls in it and allow to set further

in the refrigerator. • Store in a
cool, dry place.

Almond Clusters with Rum-Pineapple

Makes 40

85 calories per serving
Preparation time: about 35
minutes
Soaking time: about 30 minutes
Cooling time: about 2 hours

1²⁄₃ cups almonds
¾ cup dried pineapple
2 tbs white rum
Pinch ginger, freshly grated (or use ground ginger)
10 oz. milk chocolate

Scald the almonds with boiling water and leave them in
there for a few seconds. Cool
down quickly, remove the brown

skins and dry the nuts well on a
cloth. • Rinse the pineapple in a
sieve under hot water, pat dry
and cut into thin strips. • Mix
these strips with the rum and
ginger and leave to soak for
about 30 minutes. • Cut the almonds lengthways into fine
chips. • Break the chocolate into
small pieces and allow to melt in
a double boiler of very hot, but
not boiling, water, stirring occasionally. • Take the chocolate out
of the double boiler and allow to
cool to hand temperature. • Add
the almond chips and the
swollen pineapple and mix in. •
Lay a sheet of aluminum foil on
a baking tray and use two teaspoons to place small heaps of
the mixture onto it. • Leave the
tray in a cool place so that the
Almond Clusters can set. Keep
cool and dry until required.

Butter Truffles with Apricots and Pistachios

Makes 40

105 calories per serving
Preparation time: about 1 hour
Soaking time: about 30 minutes
Cooling time: about 2 hours

¾ cup dried apricots
3–4 tbs apricot liqueur
1 lb 2 oz milk chocolate
½ cup butter
Pinch salt
2 tsp carob powder
½ tsp ground cinnamon
3 tbs sour cream
1 cup pistachios, very finely chopped

Rinse off the apricots under hot water, pat thoroughly dry and cut into small pieces. Put into a small bowl. Mix with the apricot liqueur and leave to draw for about 30 minutes. • Meanwhile grate the chocolate very finely. • Put the butter into a bowl with the salt, carob and ground cinnamon, and cream until white and fluffy. • Continue stirring and gradually add the grated chocolate and sour cream; the mixture must end up light and creamy. • Mix in the softened apricots, and any alcohol which has not been absorbed, and place in the refrigerator for about 15 mintues. • If necessary, chop the pistachios a bit more, until they are only the size of a pinhead. • With cooled hands, make balls out of the truffle mixture, about the size of a walnut, roll in the pistachios and press them in lightly. • Put the Butter Truffles individually in paper cases and cool for at least 1½ hours. You must store them in a cool dry place until you want to serve them.

Marzipan-Nougat Rolls with Papaya

Makes 30

120 calories per serving
Preparation time: about 1 hour
Soaking time: about 1 hour
Cooling time: 2–3 hours

1¼ cups dried papayas
Grated rind of ½ orange
2 liquid glasses white rum
1⅔ cups almonds
1 cup honey
½ tsp vanilla extract
¾ cup nut nougat without added sugar

Rinse the papayas briefly under hot water, pat thoroughly dry and put them through a mincer, using the fine ring. (Or you can cut into small pieces.) • Then mix the papayas in a small bowl with the grated orange rind and the rum, and allow to soak, covered, for about 1 hour. • Meanwhile, scald the almonds with boiling water, remove the brown skins, and dry the nuts on a cloth. • Then purée the almonds very finely in the blender, and work to a smooth marzipan with the honey and vanilla. • Warm the nougat over a low heat until it reaches a state where it can easily be spread. • Roll out the marzipan on wax paper to a rectangle about ¼ in. thick, and spread the nougat over it. • Spread the papayas mixture onto this and roll up the marzipan with the help of the wax paper. Place in the refrigerator for 2–3 hours, then, using a sharp knife, cut into slices just ½ in. thick, and put these individually into paper cases. • You must store the Marzipan-Nougat Rolls in a cool, dry place until they are needed.

Breads and Savory Baking

Whole grain bread and rolls are not only healthier, they have a spicy and flavory taste. Let yourself be convinced—with South Tyrolean Nut Bread or Spiced Four-Grain Bread, with Spelt or Three-Grain Rolls, with flatbreads or crispbread. If you can afford more time, you should definitely try Old-fashioned Rye Bread, or Multi-grain Bread (both made with sourdough), or Spiced Mixed Bread or Rye Pretzels and Caraway. Salt Sticks are especially crispy.

The choice of spicy dishes is large, too. You will find here Tomato and Mushroom Pizza or Broccoli and Poultry Quiche, Zucchini Flan with lamb or leek, and Onion Flan with nuts, Noodle Flan with Fish and vegetables, or Lentil Pie with poultry and bean sprouts. If you prefer smaller portions, you will find Green Rye and Sage Flatbread with oyster mushrooms, Chickpea Flatbread with olives or Vegetable Turnovers with crab. And a gourmet specialty is the Potato Waffles with Herb Cream.

South Tyrolean Nutbread

375 calories per serving
Preparation time: about 45 minutes
Rising time: about 70 minutes
Baking time: about 1 hour

2¼ cups wholewheat flour, freshly ground

1½ cups buckwheat, finely ground

¼ cup fresh yeast

1 tsp honey

1½ cups warm milk

1 cup walnuts

1 cup pine nuts

⅓ cup soft butter

1½ tsp salt

1 tsp aniseeds

Wheat flour for rolling out

Butter for greasing

1 egg yolk

2 tbs heavy cream

2 tbs sunflower seeds

Mix the wheat and buckwheat flour in a bowl and make a well in the center. Put the yeast into it, together with the honey and milk, and using a little of the flour drawn from the sides, stir to a batter. Put a cloth over it and allow to ferment in a warm, draft-free place until the batter has visibly swollen and shows bubbles (at least 15 minutes). • Meanwhile, chop the walnuts semi-finely, and the pine nuts coarsely. • Roast the pine nuts in a dry pan until pale brown, then leave to cool on a plate. • Add to the dough in the well the remaining milk, the butter cut into flakes, and the salt and aniseeds, and work everything to a smooth dough. Continue to knead until it leaves the sides of the bowl clean, and bub-bles appear. • Now let the dough rise again, covered, until it has doubled in volume. • Press the dough together well and knead through on a lightly floured surface. Mix into it the walnuts and pine nuts. • Shape the dough to a round loaf and let it rise for another 20 minutes on a greased baking tray. • Preheat the oven to about 425°F. • Using a wet knife, cut slits in the top of the bread in a diamond pattern. • Whisk the egg yolk with the cream and use it to brush the bread, then sprinkle the sun-flower seeds over it. • Place the bread on the lower shelf of the hot oven and also put in a bowl of water. • After 10 minutes, re-duce the temperature to 400°F. Bake the bread for about 1 hour until golden brown and well cooked through. Place on a wire rack to cool.

Variation: South Tyrolean Nut Rolls. Prepare the dough in the same way as for the bread, but before the third rising shape into 20 round rolls and allow them to rise for only 15 minutes. Cut a cross in each one, brush with the egg yolk and cream mixture, and sprinkle sunflower or sesame seeds over them. The rolls are cooked at the same temperature, but on the middle shelf for about 35 minutes.

South Tyrolean Nut Flatbread. Add ½ cup corn flour to the wheat and buckwheat mixture. After the second rising shape the dough into good tea-plate size flatbreads. Brush them with the egg yolk and cream, and sprinkle with sunflower or sesame seeds. Without rising again, bake at the same temperature for about 20 minutes.

Spiced Four-Grain Bread

285 calories per serving
Preparation time: about 30 minutes
Rising time: about 1 hour

2¼ cups wholewheat flour

2¼ cups light rye flour

¼ cup yeast

1 cup warm water

1 tbs salt

¼ cup melted butter

1 tbs coriander

½ tsp cardamon powder

1 tsp caraway

½ cup each sesame seeds, coarse wheat groats, linseeds and sunflower seeds

Wheat flour for shaping

Butter for greasing

Mix the two flours and make sure they are at room temperature. Then make a well in the center, crumble in the yeast and stir to a dough with some water and just a little flour from the sides. Cover with a cloth and allow to ferment in a warm, draft-free place for about 15 minutes; the dough must have visibly risen and have bubbles in it. • Knead in thoroughly the remaining water with the salt, butter and spices, and allow to rise again, covered with a cloth, until it has doubled in bulk. • Then press this dough together again and knead it until it leaves the sides of the bowl and bubbles. • Mix the sesame, wheat groats and linseed and put 2 tablespoonfuls to one side. Work the remaining mixture into the dough, together with the sunflower seeds. • Shape the dough to a longish loaf with floured hands, brush it all over with warm water, sprinkle the rest of the grain mixture over it and allow to rise for another 15 minutes on a greased baking sheet. • Meanwhile, preheat the over to 400°F. • Bake the bread on the middle shelf for 60–65 minutes, cool on a wire rack, and if

possible do not cut it until the following day.

Sweet Breakfast Bread

335 calories per serving
Preparation time: about 1 hour
Rising time: at least 1¼ hours
Baking time: 45–50 minutes

2½ cups wholewheat flour, freshly ground
½ cup corn flour, finely ground
100 grams millet, finely ground
2 tbs cube yeast
½ cup warm milk
1 cup honey
2 eggs
2 egg yolks
¾ cup soft butter
Pinch salt
Pinch ground mace
2 pinches cardamon powder
Grated rind of ½ lemon
Pinch saffron powder
1 cup almonds, finely chopped
⅔ cup raisins
3 tbs rum
Wheat flour for dusting
¼ cup each candied orange and lemon peel, very finely diced
Butter for greasing
⅓ cup flaked almonds

Mix the wheat, corn and millet flours in a bowl and make a well in the center. Crumble in the yeast and stir to a dough with some milk and a little flour from the sides. • Cover the bowl with a cloth and place in a warm, draft-free place to rise, until it has clearly expanded and has bubbles. • Then add 1 cup honey, together with the eggs, egg yolks, and ½ cup butter cut into small flakes. Sprinkle the salt, mace, cardamon and grated lemon rind over it. • Dissolve the saffron in the rest of the warm milk and pour into the dough. • Work all the ingredients to a smooth dough and knead it until it leaves the sides of the bowl and has bubbles in it. Add the chopped almonds towards the end, shape the dough into a ball and leave to rise again, covered with a cloth, for at least 30 minutes, until it has doubled in bulk and the top looks "woolly." • Meanwhile, wash the raisins in a sieve in hot water and rub dry in a cloth. Put into a small bowl, pour over the rum and leave to soak, covered. • Dust the work surface thinly with wheatflour, press back the dough together and knead again. • Mix the raisins with the candied peel, dust lightly with flour and knead into the dough for a very short while. • Preheat the oven to 400°F. •

Melt about 2 teaspoons of the remaining butter over a low heat and brush the risen dough with it. Then make slits in the top with a sharp knife, making a diamond pattern, and bake the bread until light brown on the lower shelf of the hot oven for 45–50 minutes. • Take the bread out of the oven and brush immediately with the rest of the butter, which you should have melted. Let this soak in for a bit, and then brush the hot bread with the remaining honey. • Sprinkle over the almonds and let the bread cool on a wire rack.

Hazelnut Carrot Bread with Apples

240 calories per serving
Preparation time: about 1½ hours
Rising time: at least 2¼ hours
Baking time: 50–60 minutes

3½ cups wholewheat flour, freshly ground

1¼ cups millet, finely ground

1 oz cube yeast

½ cup warm water

¾ cup dried apple rings

3 tbs Calvados or rum

1¼ cups carrots

Juice of ½ lemon

⅓ cup soft butter

½ cup apple juice concentrate

1 tsp salt

Grated rind of ½ lemon

1 cup warm buttermilk

1¼ cups hazelnuts, coarsely chopped

½ cup whole oat flakes

Wheatflour for dusting and shaping

Butter for greasing

Mix the wheat and millet flour in a bowl and make a well in the center. Crumble in the yeast and stir to a batter with the warm water and a little flour from the sides. Cover with a cloth and leave to ferment for about 20 minutes in a warm, draft-free place. • In the meantime, rinse off the apple rings in a sieve under hot water, pat dry and dice very finely. Put in a small bowl together with the Calvados or rum and leave to soak, covered. • Scrape the carrots, grate coarsely and mix with the lemon juice. • Cut the soft butter into small flakes and dot around the flour at the edge of the fermented mixture. Add ½ cup apple juice concentrate, the salt, grated lemon rind and buttermilk to the mixture, and work everything to a smooth dough. Knead until it leaves the sides of the bowl and has bubbles. • Put into the dough the hazelnuts, 2 tablespoons oat flakes, the carrot and apple pieces, including any unabsorbed alcohol, and knead in thoroughly. Dust the dough lightly with flour, put a cloth over the bowl and allow the dough to rise in a warm place, until it has doubled in bulk. This takes about 1½–2 hours. • Knead the dough once more on a floured surface and shape into a longish loaf. • Place on a greased baking tray and allow to rise for another 15–20 minutes. • Preheat the oven to 400°F. • Make slits lengthways in the top of the risen bread, using a sharp knife, and sprinkle with the remaining oatflakes. • Bake the bread on the lower shelf of the hot oven for 50–60 minutes, and place on a wire rack. Spread the rest of the apple juice concentrate on the loaf while it is still hot, and allow the bread to cool completely before cutting. Serve as fresh as possible, as that is when it tastes best.

Variation: Walnut Carrot Bread with Pears. For this, replace the hazelnuts with walnuts and use dried pears instead of dried apples, which you should soak in pear liqueur. You would also do better to use pear juice concentrate instead of apple. Bake this bread sprinkled with very finely chopped walnuts, too, or in a loaf pan lined with nuts. Brush the top of the bread after rising with some warm water, and decorate with walnut halves, if you wish. Give the top additional glaze by spreading it with pear juice concentrate after baking.

Ricotta and Raisin Rolls

255 calories per serving
Preparation time: about 40 minutes
Rising time: at least 1 hour
Baking time: 20–25 minutes

2¼ cups wholewheat flour, freshly ground

½ cup buckwheat flour

¼ cup fresh yeast

---

5 tbs warm milk

⅓ cup soft butter

---

2 cups ricotta cheese

½ cup honey

---

2 eggs

Pinch salt

Grated rind of ½ lemon

---

1 cup raisins

---

2 liqueur glasses cognac or rum

Wheatflour for dusting and shaping

Butter for greasing

---

1 egg yolk

---

2 tbs cream or milk

---

2 tbs each poppy and sesame seeds

Mix the wheat and buckwheat flour in a bowl, make a well in the center and crumble the yeast into it. Stir in the warm milk and a little flour from the sides and leave to ferment, covered with a cloth, in a warm, draft-free place until it forms bubbles. • Cut the soft butter into small flakes and, together with the cheese (drained if necessary), the honey and the eggs, add it to the yeast mixture. Season with the salt and grated lemon rind, and work everything to a smooth dough. Knead until it comes away from the edges of the bowl and forms bubbles. • Place a cloth over the bowl and let the dough rise for at least 30 minutes; it must double in volume and the top should look "woolly." • Meanwhile, wash the raisins in a sieve under hot water and rub well in a cloth to dry. Pour the cognac or rum over the raisins in a small bowl and leave to soak, covered. • Dust the work surface with flour. • Press back together the risen dough and knead thoroughly on the floured surface. At the end, add the raisins. • Grease a baking tray with butter. • Using floured hands, make balls about 2 in. in diameter out of the dough, and place next to each other on the baking sheet, leaving sufficient room around them. Let them rise again for about 15 minutes. • Whisk the egg yolk with the cream or milk, and brush all the rolls with it, but sprinkle half with poppy seeds and the other half with sesame seeds. • Place the sheet on the middle shelf of the hot oven, and bake for 20–25 minutes until light brown. • Place the rolls on a wire rack, let them cool and serve as fresh as possible, as they dry out rather quickly.

Buckwheat Rolls with Onion

Makes 15

75 calories per serving
Preparation time: about 40 minutes
Rising time: at least 1 hour
Baking time: 25–30 minutes

---

3 cups buckwheat flour, freshly ground

---

1 cup green rye

---

1 oz cube yeast

---

1 cup warm milk

¼ tsp each marjoram and lovage, very finely grated

½ tsp salt

---

1 egg

| ¾ cup onion |
| 2 tbs butter |
| White pepper, freshly ground |
| Wheatflour for dusting |
| Butter for greasing |
| 1 egg yolk |
| 2 tbs cream |
| Caraway seeds for decorating |

Mix the buckwheat and green rye flour in a bowl, make a well in the center and crumble the yeast into it. Stir to a batter with some milk and a little flour drawn from the sides, and allow to ferment, covered, for about 15 minutes. • Add the marjoram, lovage, salt, egg and remaining milk and work everything to a smooth dough. Knead until it leaves the sides of the bowl and has bubbles. Allow to rise to double its size for at least 30 minutes. • In the meantime, peel the onion and dice finely and fry in the heated butter until

it becomes transparent. Put in the pepper and salt if you wish, and allow to cool. • Knead the dough on a floured surface, work the onion into it and shape the dough to balls about the size of an egg. Make a slit in the top of each roll, place on a greased baking sheet, leaving sufficient room around them and let them rise again. • Preheat the oven to 350°F. • Whisk the egg yolk with the cream and brush the rolls with it. Sprinkle the caraway over them and bake on the middle shelf of the hot oven for 25–30 minutes.

Three-Grain Rolls with Linseeds

Makes 20

125 calories per servings
Preparation time: about 35 minutes
Rising time: at least 1 hour

Baking time: 35–40 minutes

| 2½ cups wholewheat flour, freshly ground |
| 1¾ cups rye, finely ground |
| 1 cup buckwheat, finely ground |
| 1 oz cube yeast |
| 1 cup warm water |
| 2 tsp salt |
| ½ tsp each caraway and coriander, finely ground |
| Pinch fennel, freshly ground |
| ½ cup linseeds |
| Wheat flour for dusting and shaping |
| Butter for greasing |
| 1 egg yolk |
| 2 tbs milk or water |

Mix all the types of flour, make a well in the center, and crumble the yeast into it, with some water and a little flour drawn from the sides. Stir to a batter and let it ferment, covered, for about 20 minutes. •

Add the rest of the water, together with the salt, caraway, coriander and fennel, and work everything to a smooth dough. Knead until it leaves the sides of the bowl and has bubbles. • Finally, knead in about ½ cup linseeds and allow the dough to rise for at least 30 minutes, covered with a cloth again. • Then knead thoroughly again on a floured surface, shape in 20 round rolls and cut a cross in the top of each. Lay them on a greased baking sheet and let them rise for the last time, about 15 minutes. • Whisk the egg yolks with the milk or water, brush the rolls with them, sprinkle on the remaining linseeds and place on the middle shelf of the oven. Place a shallow oven-proof dish with water on the floor of the oven, turn to 400°F—425°F and bake the rolls for 35–40 minutes.

Whole Grain Brioches

Makes 20

205 calories per serving
Preparation time: about 1 hour
Rising time: 15–20 hours
Baking time: about 15 minutes

¼ cup yeast
5 tbs warm milk
3 cups wholewheat flour, freshly ground
1 cup millet, finely ground
5 eggs
2 tbs honey
1½ tsp salt
Wheatflour for dusting and shaping
1¼ cups soft butter
Butter for greasing
1 egg yolk
2 tbs cream

Crumble the yeast into a cup, stir with the milk and leave to rest in a warm place for about 10 minutes. • Mix the wheat and millet flour in a bowl and make a well in the center. • Beat the eggs with the honey and salt and pour into the well, together with the milk and yeast. • Stir the ingredients to a smooth dough, working from the middle out. • Put a couple of tablespoons of wheatflour in a sieve and dust the work surface with it (use the bran left behind elsewhere). • Put the dough, which should be really soft, onto the flour. Sieve some more wheatflour over it, and then knead everything until the dough is no longer sticky. It is best to use only one hand for kneading, and with the other to constantly push the dough together with a dough scraper, sieving some flour over it now and again. • When the dough is smooth and elastic, cut the butter into small flakes and gradually knead into the dough. Work as quickly as possible, so that the butter does not become too soft and make the dough sticky again. • Shape the dough into a ball, sieve some wheatflour over it, and lay a large sheet of plastic wrap over it. • Let the dough rest at room temperature for 3½–4 hours, until it has doubled or tripled in size. • Sieve flour over the work surface again and knead the dough through vigorously. • Then put it back into the bowl, dust with flour, cover with plastic wrap and leave it to rest overnight in the refrigerator. • The next day, carefully grease 20 brioche pans (or tart pans with high edges). • Knead through the dough again on a floured surface, and divide into 20 pieces of equal size. • Take away one-third of the dough from each piece. • Shape the larger pieces into smooth balls, and place each one in a brioche pan. Use your thumb to make a hollow in the dough, then shape the smaller pieces into balls and place them in the hollows. • Cover the brioches with a cloth and leave to rise for another 15 minutes. • In the meantime, preheat the oven to 425°F. Whisk the egg yolk with the cream. • Brush the brioches with the egg mixture, place on a baking tray or the metal oven shelf and bake on the middle shelf of the hot oven. Bake for about 15 minutes until light brown, and then let them cool a while next to the oven. Take the brioches out of the pans, leave to cool on a wire rack, and serve fresh.

Yogurt and Millet Crispbread

Makes 32

45 calories per serving
Preparation time: about 35 minutes
Soaking time: about 1 hour
Baking time: 15–20 minutes

1¾ cups millet, finely ground

1½ cups wholewheat flour, freshly ground

½ tsp salt

¼ tsp caraway, freshly ground

2 pinches cardamon, freshly ground

1 cup warm water

3 tbs creamy plain yogurt

2 tbs sunflower oil

Oil for brushing

Wheatflour for rolling out

Butter for greasing

Mix the millet and wheatflour in a bowl with the salt, caraway and cardamon, and make a well in the center. • Pour in the water, together with the yogurt and oil and work everything to a smooth dough. Now knead it until it becomes firm and elastic. This is best done with the dough hook of a hand electric mixer. • Brush the dough with some oil and leave to rest for about 1 hour under a hot pan, so that the flour can swell. • Sieve some flour onto the surface. • Preheat the oven to 400°F. • Generously grease a baking sheet. • Divide the dough into 8 pieces and roll them out to ¼ in. thick. Cut each piece into quarters and place on the baking sheet. • Bake immediately on the middle shelf of the hot oven for 15–20 minutes, until light brown and crispy, and allow to cool on a wire rack.

Rye Crispbread with Bran

Makes 32

45 calories per serving
Preparation time: about 45 minutes
Soaking time: about 1½ hours
Baking time: 15–20 minutes

1¾ cups rye, finely ground

1½ cups wholewheat flour, freshly ground

½ tsp salt

½ tsp caraway, freshly ground

2 pinches fennel, freshly ground

½ cup warm water

3 tbs warm buttermilk

3 tbs sunflower oil

Oil for brushing

Wheatflour for rolling out

Butter for greasing

Warm water for sprinkling

Sieve the rye flour and keep back the bran. • Mix the fine rye flour in a bowl with the wheat flour, the salt, caraway and fennel, make a well in the center and put in the water together with the buttermilk and oil. • Work the dough as in the previous recipe, kneading it for at least 15–20 minutes, allowing it 1½ hours to rise. • Sieve the flour for rolling out, and use the bran elsewhere. • Roll out the dough as in the first recipe, cut and lay on a greased baking sheet. • Brush the tops with some warm water and sprinkle the rye-bran over them. • Bake them similarly for 15–20 minutes in an oven heated to 400°F.

Tip: You can sprinkle the crispbread with sesame, poppy or caraway seeds instead of bran. All types of crispbread should always be kept cool and dry until needed.

Cheese Sticks

Makes 30

110 calories per serving
Preparation time: about 1 hour
Rising time: at least 1¼ hours
Baking time: 25-30 minutes

2½ cups buckwheat, finely ground

1¾ cups millet, finely ground

1 oz. cube yeast

½ cup warm water

¼ cup soft butter

2 tbs. creamy plain yogurt

1 egg

1 egg white

1 tsp. salt

1 tbs. paprika powder

1¼ cups Emmental cheese, freshly grated

½ cup Parmesan cheese, freshly grated

1 egg yolk

2 tbs. milk

Butter for greasing

Wheatflour for rolling out and shaping

Put 2 flours in a bowl, crumble in the yeast, and mix with the water and some flour drawn from the sides, stir to a batter and allow to ferment for 15 minutes. • Cut the butter into small flakes and mix with the yogurt, egg, egg white, salt and paprika. Work everything to a smooth dough. • Knead until it has bubbles and leaves the sides of the bowl. • Allow to rise for about an hour to double its volume. • In between, mix 1 cup Emmental with the Parmesan, whisk the egg yolk with the milk, and grease a baking sheet. • Knead the pastry through, divide into 30 pieces and roll out each one to an oval about ¼ in. thick. Brush with some egg yolk, and sprinkle with the cheese mixture.

Roll into sticks from the long side, and press the ends together. • Preheat the oven to 425°F. • Brush the Cheese Sticks on the sheet with the remaining egg yolk, and sprinkle with the Emmental. Bake on the middle shelf for 25-30 minutes, and then let them cool on a wire rack.

Green Rye Rolls with Linseeds and Poppy Seeds

Makes 20

150 calories per serving
Preparation time: about 1 hour
Resting time: about 4¾ hours
Baking time: 25-30 minutes

1¾ cups rye, finely ground

4 oz. sourdough (from the recipe) from the baker or ready-packaged)

2 cups warm water

1¾ cups wholewheat flour, finely ground

2¼ cups green rye, finely ground

1 cup linseeds, freshly pounded

1 oz. cube yeast

1 tbs. salt

Wheatflour, finely ground, for kneading and shaping

Butter for greasing

Water for brushing

¼ cup linseeds

¼ cup poppy seeds

Put the rye flour in a bowl and make a well in the center. Stir the sourdough with about three-quarters of the water, mix into the flour, and leave to rest in a warm place for about 4 hours. • Mix the wheat and green rye flour with the linseed groats and put into the sourdough mixture. Dissolve the yeast in the rest of the water and

add with the salt. • Work everything to a smooth dough, and knead until it leaves the sides of the bowl and has bubbles in it. Leave to rise for about 30 minutes, covered with a cloth. • Knead the dough thoroughly on a floured surface and shape into 20 balls of equal size. • Lay these on a greased baking sheet and let them rise for another 15 minutes, allowing them to "grow together" a bit. • Preheat the oven to 425°F. • Brush the rolls with water, sprinkle over the linseeds and poppy seeds. • Place the sheet on the middle shelf of the hot oven, and bake the rolls for 25-30 minutes, then allow to cool on a wire rack.

Oat Rolls with Nuts

Makes 12

210 calories per serving
Preparation time: about 1½ hours

Time for soaking and roasting: about 2½ hours
Rising time: at least 1¼ hours
Baking time: 35-40 minutes

½ cup ground soybeans
1 cup warm water
1 cup whole oats
1¾ cups wheat
½ cup rye
1 tsp. coriander
1 oz. cube yeast
Wheatflour for dusting and shaping
1 cup hazelnuts, flaked or coarsely chopped
Water for brushing
Butter for greasing

Let the ground soybean soak for about 1 hour in 1¾ pints water. • Preheat the oven to 200°F. • Roast the whole oats on a baking tray for about 1 hour, and cool on a plate. • Then grind finely with the wheat, rye and coriander and put into a bowl. • Make a well in the center, crumble in the yeast and with the rest of the water and some flour drawn from the sides, stir to a batter. Let it ferment for about 15 minutes, covered with a cloth. • Add the yogurt, ground soybean and salt, work everything to a smooth dough and knead until it leaves the sides of the bowl and has bubbles in it. Let it rise again for 1 hour. • Knead the dough through, mix in ⅔ cup hazelnuts and make 12 longish rolls. Slit these once lengthways, brush with water and sprinkle with the remaining nuts. • Put into a cold oven on a greased baking sheet. • Turn the heat to 425°F. Once it has reached that temperature, bake the rolls for another 35-40 minutes.

Soy Flatbread with Garlic and Herbs

Makes 20

160 calories per serving
Preparation time: about 1 hour
Rising time: at least 1¼ hours
Baking time: 20-25 minutes

4½ cups wholewheat flour, freshly ground
1½ cups soybeans, ground to flour
½ cup soybeans, pounded to groats
1 oz. cube yeast
2 tsp. honey
2 cups warm buttermilk
2-3 garlic cloves
¼ cup butter
1 tbs. green pepper (from a jar)
1 tbs. dried thyme
1 tbs. dried oregano
½ cup warm water

Wheatflour for dusting and shaping

Butter for greasing

Mix the wheatflour with the soy flour and groats in a bowl and make a well in the center. Crumble in the yeast and stir to a batter with the honey, buttermilk and some flour drawn from the sides. Allow to ferment for about 15 minutes in a warm place. • Meanwhile, peel and dice the garlic, fry until transparent in moderately hot butter, and allow to cool. • Drain and chop the green pepper. • Add the garlic with the butter, pepper and herbs to the batter and work to a smooth dough with the water and the rest of the flour. Knead until it leaves the sides of the bowl and has bubbles in it. • Leave to rise for 45 minutes. • Knead the dough vigorously, di-

vide into 20 pieces and press into small flatbreads. Place on a greased baking tray and allow to rise for another 15 minutes. • Preheat the oven to 425°F. • Bake the flatbreads on the middle shelf for 15-20 minutes until golden brown.

Multi-Grain Bread

450 calories per serving
Preparation time: about 1 hour
Resting time altogether: about 8 hours
Baking time: about 1¾ hours

2½ cups wholewheat flour, freshly ground
1 cup rye, finely ground
6 oz. sourdough (from the recipe) from the baker or ready-packaged
4 cups warm water
1 cup soy groats

1 cup each millet, barley, corn and oats, all finely ground
1 oz. cube yeast
1 tbs. salt
2 tbs. honey
5 tbs. corn oil
½ cup linseeds, coarsely pounded
½ cup sunflower or pumpkin seeds
Wheatflour for kneading and shaping
Butter for greasing
Water for brushing and baking

Mix the wheat and rye flour in a bowl. Stir the sourdough with about 2 cups warm water, work into the flour mixture and leave to rise, covered with a cloth, in a warm place for about 6 hours. • After about 5 hours stir the soy groats in a bowl with 1 cup warm water and leave to soak, covered with a

cloth, for 1 hour. • Mix the millet, barley, corn and oat flour together, shaking them a bit so that they can aerate. • Dissolve the yeast in the remaining warm water and work into the flour together with the salt, honey, wheat or corn oil and the sourdough mixture. Add as well the soaked soy groats. • Set aside 1 tablespoon each of the linseeds and the sunflower or pumpkin seeds. Mix the rest into the dough. Dust with some wheatflour, cover with a cloth and leave to rest for about 30 minutes. • Dust the work surface with flour and knead the dough thoroughly on it. Shape into a ball. Put back into the bowl, sprinkle with some flour and let it rise for another 45 minutes. • Now knead the dough through again on the floured surface, shape into a loaf and place on a greased baking sheet. Let it have

a final 45 minutes to rise. •
Preheat the oven to 500°F. •
Press the risen dough back into
shape a bit, brush with water,
and sprinkle with the rest of the
linseeds and sunflower or pumpkin seeds. • Put the baking sheet
on the lower shelf of the hot
oven, also a bowl of boiling
water, and pour some water on
the oven floor. • After 15 minutes turn down the heat to 375°F
and bake the loaf for a further
1½ hours. • Test the loaf by
knocking it on the underside
with your fingers: if it sounds
hollow, the bread is cooked
through and should be put to
cool on a wire rack.

Barley Rolls with Mushroom Flavor

Makes 12

185 calories per serving
Preparation time: about 1½
hours
Soaking time: about 1 hour
Time for swelling, cooling and
rising: nearly 3 hours
Baking time: 25-30 minutes

2 tbs. dried button mushrooms
2 cups warm water
1 shallot
1 cup whole barley coarsely ground
2 tbs. butter
Salt
Freshly ground white pepper
3½ cups wholewheat flour, freshly ground
1 oz. cube yeast
½ cup warm milk
Bunch parsley
2-3 sprigs thyme
Wheatflour for kneading and shaping
2 tbs. cream
1 egg yolk
Butter for greasing

Allow the mushrooms to soak
in the water for about 1
hour. • Pour the water from the
mushrooms through a filter paper, to remove any dirt. • Peel
the shallots, dice, and fry in the
butter with the barley groats. •
Pour over the mushroom water,
bring to a boil, add salt and pepper and leave, covered, over a
low heat for 30 minutes for the
ingredients to swell, then allow to
cool. • Put the flour in a bowl,
make a well in the center and
crumble in the yeast. Stir with
the milk and some flour drawn
from the sides and allow to ferment for 15 minutes. • Rinse off
the parsley and thyme, pat dry
and, together with the mushrooms, chop finely. • Put into the
bowl with the cooled barley and
work everything to a smooth
dough. Knead until bubbles appear. Leave to rise for about 1
hour. • Knead the dough
through vigorously, remove
pieces about the size of an egg,
and shape into round rolls. Use
scissors to cut into the tops in a
starshape, and then brush with
the egg yolk, whisked with the
cream. • Place on a greased baking sheet on the middle shelf of
a cold oven. Turn the heat to
425°F and once it has reached
the right temperature bake for a
further 25-30 minutes, then allow to cool.

Pretzels

Makes 12

170 calories per serving
Preparation time: about 1 hour
Rising time: about 2 hours
Baking time: 20-25 minutes

5 cups wholewheat flour, freshly ground
1 oz. cube yeast
6 cups warm water
1-2 tsp. salt
Wheatflour for rolling out and shaping
Butter for greasing
2 tbs. baking soda
Coarse salt for decoration

Aerate the wheatflour well in a bowl, make a well in the center and crumble in the yeast. Add about 1¾ pints warm water and stir the yeast to a batter with it and some flour drawn from the sides. Cover with a cloth and let the batter rest for about 10 minutes. • Meanwhile, dissolve the salt in 1 cup water. • Mix the rest of the flour, together with the saltwater, into the batter and knead vigorously for about 10 minutes on a floured surface, until it is elastic and comes away from the surface easily. • Shape the dough into a ball, replace in the bowl and cover with a damp cloth, so that the top does not dry out. Allow to rise for about 1½ hours at room temperature. • Grease a baking sheet with butter. • Knead the dough through well on the newly-floured surface, shape into an even roll and divide into 12 pieces. • Pull each piece into a strand about 20 in. long, which is thinner at the ends than in the middle. Keep the other pieces of dough covered with a damp cloth while doing this. • Put the finished strand of dough together in a pretzel twist, making sure the ends are pressed down. • Bring the rest of the water to a boil in a wide, shallow pan, and dissolve the baking soda in it. • Lay the pretzels in the water a couple at a time, and let them draw in there for about ½ minute. You must baste them constantly with the water, or press them lightly under the surface. • Preheat the oven to 425°F. • After they have been dipped in the water, place the pretzels on the greased tray, and sprinkle with the coarse salt. • Place the tray on the middle shelf of the hot oven, and bake the pretzels for 20-25 minutes until brown and crispy. • Allow to cool on a wire rack.

Variation: Caraway Salt Sticks. For these, prepare the dough in exactly the same way as the rye pretzels, only grind in some car-away with the wheatflour. After the resting time divide the dough into 12 pieces and, using a thin rolling-pin, roll them one after the other to flat ovals, about ¼ in. thick. Now hold down one of the narrow sides and roll up the dough with the other hand. Press the ends of the dough together well and then immerse the sticks into the baking soda water in the same way as the pretzels. Lay them on a greased baking sheet, sprinkle with a mixture of car-away and coarse salt and bake for about 35 minutes on the middle shelf of a very hot oven (425°F). Here too the other dough must rest under a damp cloth, while the sticks are being shaped and immersed in the water.

Rye Rolls

Makes 15

110 calories per serving
Preparation time: about 1½ hours
Resting time: about 3½ hours
Baking time: 30-40 minutes

/2 oz. yeast

1½ cups warm water

4 oz. sourdough (from the recipe) from the baker, or ready-packaged)

3½ cups rye, finely ground

½ cup wholewheat flour, freshly ground

1 tbs. salt

1 tbs. caraway

Rye-flour or wheatflour for dusting, kneading and shaping

Butter for greasing

Water for brushing and baking

Caraway for decorating

Dissolve the yeast in the warm water and stir the sourdough into it, until it has dissolved too. • Mix the wheat and rye flour together, stir half of it into the sourdough mixture and leave everything to rest for about 3 hours in a warm place, covered with a cloth. • Mix the rest of the flour well with the salt and caraway in a bowl. Put the first dough, now risen, in as well and mix everything well together. Then knead the dough until it leaves the sides of the bowl and has bubbles in it. Dust the work surface with flour and knead the dough on it very thoroughly until it is elastic and no longer sticky. Dust a baking tray or a plate with flour. • Divide the dough into 15 pieces of equal size, shape them into smooth balls and set them on the baking tray, leaving space around them. Put a cloth over them and allow

to rise for 20-30 minutes, until they have grown visibly taller and the tops look "woolly". • Preheat the oven to 425°F and grease a baking tray with butter. Put the rolls on the tray, brush with warm water and sprinkle with caraway. If desired, cut into them in a star or cross shape with a very sharp knife, and place on the middle shelf of the hot oven. • At the same time, put a bowl of boiling water into the oven and pour some water on the hot oven floor. Shut the door immediately, so that the steam cannot escape, otherwise the dough will be forced upwards. • Bake the rolls for 30-40 minutes until crispy brown, and allow to cool on a wire rack.

Tip: As the quantity of dough is enough for 2 baking trays, you should cover the second tray with a cloth, and put it in a cool

place, until the oven is free again. With a fan-assisted oven both trays can of course be put in at the same time.

Variation: Spiced Mixed Grain Rye Rolls. Stir together half of a 1 oz. cube of yeast with the water, 2 oz. sourdough and 1¼ cups each rye and wheat flour (both freshly ground), and leave to rise, covered with a cloth. Mix 1¼ cups each rye and wheat flour with 1 tablespoon each salt, caraway and coriander, 1 teaspoon fennel or aniseed and 2 tablespoons sesame seeds. Add the yeast dough to it, knead as described above, and form into rolls. After the rising, brush likewise with water and sprinkle with sesame seeds, or poppy seeds, and bake until crispy brown. Allow to cool on a wire rack.

Green Rye and Sage Flatbread with Oyster Mushrooms

Makes 8

345 calories per serving
Preparation time: about 1 hour
Rising time: at least 45 minutes
Baking time: 15-20 minutes

| 2½ cups green rye, finely ground |
| 1¾ cups wholewheat flour, freshly ground |
| 1 oz. cube yeast |
| 1 tsp. honey |
| ½ cup warm milk |
| ¾ cup oyster mushrooms |
| 1-2 cloves garlic |
| 2 tbs. butter |
| Salt |
| Black pepper, freshly ground |
| 4-5 sprigs sage |
| 5 tbs. buttermilk |
| 1 egg |
| Pinch cayenne pepper |
| ⅓ cup pumpkin seeds |
| Wheatflour for kneading and shaping |
| Butter for greasing |
| 1 egg yolk |

Mix the green rye and wheat flour in a bowl, make a well in the center and crumble in the yeast. Add the honey and some milk and, with some flour drawn from the sides, work everything to a batter. Place a cloth over it and allow to rest for about 15 minutes, until it has clearly risen and shows bubbles. • In the meantime, clean the oyster mushrooms and chop finely. • Peel the garlic, dice very finely and fry in the butter with the mushrooms, stirring continuously until they are steaming. Season with salt and pepper. • Rinse the sage, dry off and cut into thin strips. • Mix into the mushrooms and fry them briefly together. Allow everything to cool. • Add the remaining milk, the buttermilk, egg and cayenne pepper to the batter, and work everything to a smooth dough.

Knead until it shows bubbles. •
Put the cloth back over the
dough, and let it rise for 30 minutes, until it has nearly doubled
in volume. • Finely chop half of
the pumpkin seeds. • Dust the
work surface with flour, knead
the dough through on it, mixing
in the chopped seeds with the
mushroom mixture. • Divide the
dough into 8 pieces. On a
floured surface, press each one
flat to about the size of a saucer.
• Place them on a lightly greased
baking tray. • Preheat the oven
to 425°F. • Brush the flatbreads,
which should have meanwhile
risen slightly, with the whisked
egg yolk, and sprinkle them with
the rest of the pumpkin seeds.
Place the tray on the middle
shelf of the hot oven, and bake
the flatbread for 15-20 minutes.
• Leave to cool and serve fresh.

Variation: Chickpea Flatbread
with Olives. Soak ⅔ cups
chickpeas, covered with water,
overnight. Then boil them in
the same water for 3½ hours,
together with 2 peeled onions,
1-2 peeled cloves garlic and 2
peeled and coarsely diced carrots. Pass through a sieve and
allow to cool. Put 1¾ cups
freshly ground wholewheat
flour in a bowl and make a
batter with 1 oz. yeast, 1 teaspoon honey and some milk.
Allow to rise. Knead in the
chickpea purée with the rest of
the milk (½ cup in total) and
2 tablespoons tomato purée,
and allow to rise for 30 minutes. Finely chop 2 bunches of
parsley, ½ cup olives and 1 tablespoon capers, and knead
into the dough with salt, pepper and cayenne pepper.
Shape into flatbreads, brush
with egg yolk and bake. Sprinkle with coarsely ground pepper.

Tomato and Mushroom Pizza

1205 calories per serving
Preparation time: about 1½
hours
Rising time: about 45 minutes
Baking time: about 20 minutes

For the dough:
2½ cups wholewheat flour, freshly ground
1½ cups rye, finely ground
½ cup linseeds, coarsely ground
1 oz. cube yeast
1 cup buttermilk, at room temperature
1 egg
½ tsp. salt
¼ tsp. dried oregano, grated
4 tbs. olive oil, cold-pressed
For the topping:
1 lb. 2 oz. large ripe tomatoes
3 onions

2 cloves garlic
6 tbs. olive oil, cold-pressed
Salt
Black pepper, freshly ground
1 tsp. honey
Cayenne pepper
3 sprigs oregano
3¼ cups champignon mushrooms
Juice of 1 lemon
1 bunch parsley
1 bunch basil
3 tbs. freshly grated Parmesan cheese
2-2½ cups mozzarella

Mix the wheat and rye flour
in a bowl with the ground
linseeds, and make a well in the
center. Crumble in the yeast, stir
to a batter with a little buttermilk
and some flour drawn from the
sides, and leave to ferment, covered for about 15 minutes. •

Then add the rest of the buttermilk, the egg, salt, oregano and olive oil and knead everything to a very smooth, elastic, dough; if needed, add some water as well, a drop at a time. • Allow the dough to rise for at least 30 minutes, covered with a cloth. • Meanwhile, scald the tomatoes with boiling water, cool them down with cold water and skin. • Remove the bases of the stalks and cores, and chop the stalks finely. • Peel the onions and the garlic cloves. Dice 1 onion very finely, cut the other into thin rings. Chop the garlic similarly into small cubes. • Heat 1 tablespoon olive oil in a wide pan and fry the diced onion until it is transparent. Add half of the garlic with the chopped tomatoes and season with salt, pepper, the honey and cayenne pepper. Bring to a boil uncovered and continue to cook until it is

slightly thicker. • Rinse the oregano, spin it dry and put the leaves of 1 sprig into the sauce. • Clean the mushrooms, wash if necessary and dry thoroughly, then cut into flakes. Mix immediately with the lemon juice. • Heat about 2 tablespoons olive oil in a large pan and fry the onion rings in it, stirring, until they are transparent. Add the mushrooms and fry, turning carefully, until nearly all the exuded juices have steamed off. • Rinse the parsley and basil, pat dry, and chop the parsley finely. Add the latter to the mushrooms, together with the rest of the garlic and the leaves of the second sprig of oregano. Season with salt, pepper and cayenne pepper, and remove the pan from the heat. • Taste the tomato sauce and adjust the seasoning, and remove from the heat as well. • Grease a baking tray with some oil. •

Knead the dough through once more, divide into 4 pieces, roll out into flat circles and allow to rise until the tomato sauce and the mushroom mixture are no longer hot. • Preheat the oven to 400°F. • Spread the tomato sauce over the dough circles, pluck off the basil leaves and sprinkle over. Distribute the mushroom mixture on top of this and sprinkle over the remaining oregano leaves and the parmesan cheese. • Cut the mozzarella into thin slices. Spread them on the topping and dribble over the rest of the olive oil. • Bake the pizzas for about 20 minutes on the middle shelf of the oven.

Broccoli and Chicken Quiche

1035 calories per serving
Preparation time: about 1½ hours
Cooling time: about 1 hour
Baking time: about 30 minutes

1 cup cashew nuts
1 tsp. salt
1¾ cups wholewheat flour, freshly ground
½ cup green rye, finely ground
½ cup Emmental cheese, freshly grated
½ cup chilled butter
1 egg
2-3 tbs. ice-cold water
1 lb. 2 oz. chicken breasts, boned and skinned
1 tbs. soy sauce
2 tbs. dry sherry
White pepper, freshly ground

| Cayenne pepper |
| 2¼ cups broccoli |
| 1 tbs. oil |
| 1 red pepper |
| Wheatflour for rolling out |
| Butter for greasing |
| 4 cups heavy cream |
| 2 egg yolks |
| 1 carton (6 oz.) creamy plain yogurt |
| 2 dashes Worcestershire sauce |

Roast the cashew nuts in a dry pan until pale brown, mixing in the salt at the end. Then allow the nuts to cool completely. • Next chop the nuts coarsely, put into a plastic bag and crush them as finely as possible with a rolling-pin. • Mix half of the nuts with the wheatflour, ½ cup green rye flour and ¼ cup cheese, put onto the work surface and make a well in the center. • Cut the butter into small flakes and dot around the edge of the flour. • Break the egg into the middle and knead all the ingredients very quickly to a smooth dough, adding the ice cold water a drop at a time. • Shape the dough into a ball and place, covered, in the refrigerator for 1 hour. • In the meantime, pat the chicken breasts dry, cut into strips across the fibers, and place in a small bowl. Pour over the soy sauce and the sherry and season with some pepper and cayenne pepper. Allow to marinate, stirring several times. • Remove the large leaves and woody parts of the stalks from the broccoli. Then divide into equal-size florets, peel off the stalks and cut into sticks. • Blanch the broccoli for 2-3 minutes in fast-boiling, salted water, cool down with ice-cold water and drain very thoroughly. • Heat the oil in a pan and brown the poultry pieces very quickly, a portion at a time. When each is done, remove from the pan and place on one side in a sieve. • Remove the stalks, membranes and pips from the red pepper, rinse in cold water and dry. Then cut into strips about ¼ in. wide and 1 in. long. • Preheat the oven to 425°F. • Roll out the pastry on a lightly floured surface. • Grease an 11 in. diameter spring-release pan and line with the pastry, making a rim about 1½ in. high. Prick the base several times with a fork. • Mix the broccoli with the chicken and red pepper strips and put into the pastry case. • Whip the cream until stiff. • Beat together very thoroughly the remaining green rye flour, the egg yolks and the yogurt and season to a good spicy taste with the salt, pepper, cayenne pepper and Worcestershire sauce. Mix in the rest of the cashew nuts together with the rest of the cheese and finally fold in the cream. Spread this mixture over the filling and place the quiche immediately on the lower shelf of the hot oven. • Bake for about 30 minutes, until the cream mixture is firm, but only lightly browned. If it browns too quickly, cover the top with a sheet of baking parchment or aluminum foil. • Serve the quiche immediately, as it tastes best when warm.

Herring and Cabbage Flan

8 pieces

595 calories per serving
Preparation time: about 45 minutes
Soaking time: about 30 minutes
Baking time altogether: about 40 minutes

9 cups floury potatoes

Salt

White pepper, freshly ground

Nutmeg, freshly grated

1¼ cups buckwheat, finely ground

5 eggs

1 bunch dill

2¼ lbs. savoy cabbage

3 carrots

Oil for greasing

2 onions

2 cooking apples

Juice of ½ lemon

8 white herring filets

2¼ cups cream

1¼ cups sour cream

1-2 tsp. hot mustard

Peel, wash and dry the potatoes and grate finely, using a grater or food-processor. Press in a cloth, season with salt, pepper and nutmeg and carefully stir in the buckwheat flour together with 3 eggs. • Rinse the dill, spin it dry and chop very finely. Mix into the dough, and stand it on one side, covered with a cloth, so that the flour can swell. • Clean the cabbage, cut into fine strips, like shavings, wash in a sieve and allow to drain. • Peel the carrots and cut into chips as thin as matches. • Bring plenty of lightly salted water to a boil in a saucepan, cook the carrot chips in it for 4 minutes, then cool down with cold water and drain. • Then put the cabbage into a boiling water, blanch for 2 minutes, cool down similarly and drain thoroughly. • Preheat the oven to 475°F. • Grease a deep baking tray or a very large quiche pan with oil, spread the potato-dough smoothly into it, and bake for about 15 minutes on the middle shelf of the hot oven. • Meanwhile, peel the onions and the apples. Cut the onions into thin rings, core the apples and grate coarsely, mixing immediately with the lemon juice. • Cut the herring filets crossways into narrow strips. • Beat the cream with the sour cream and remaining eggs, and season with salt, pepper and mustard, enough to give it a good spicy taste. • Mix all the prepared ingredients gently together, turn down the oven heat to 400°F and take out the pre-baked pastry case. • Spread the cabbage mixture onto the case and bake the flan for a further 25 minutes until golden brown. Serve hot.

Variation: Sauerkraut Flan with Herring. This flan tastes especially piquant if you replace the cabbage with sauerkraut. However, you must of course then allow somewhat longer for preparation, as it is recommended to stew the sauerkraut in the usual way before spreading it on the baked flan-case. Otherwise it will be rather coarse and hard, and therefore not as easily digestible.

Potato Waffles with Cucumber and Herb Cream

Makes 6

350 calories per serving
Preparation time: 30-35 minutes
Baking time: about 3 minutes

4½ cups floury potatoes

2 onions

2 eggs

1 egg yolk

½ cup linseeds, coarsely ground

Salt

White pepper, freshly ground

1¼ cups cream

1¼ cups creamy plain yogurt

1 tsp. honey

Juice of ½ lemon

1-2 tsp. mustard

1-2 tsp. horseradish, freshly grated

2-3 dashes Worcestershire sauce

½ salad cucumber

1-2 cloves garlic

2 hardboiled eggs

2 gherkin pickles

½ bunch dill

½ bunch parsley

½ bunch chives

Oil for greasing

Peel the potatoes and onions. Wash the potatoes, dry thoroughly, and grate or process with the onions. Squeeze out in a cloth and stir well with the eggs, egg yolks, and linseeds. Season with salt and pepper and allow to soak, covered, while you prepare the cucumber and herb cream. • For this, beat together thoroughly the cream with the yogurt, honey and lemon juice until light and creamy. Stir in the mustard, horseradish and Worcestershire sauce. • Brush off the cucumber thoroughly in cold water and dry off. Then grate into fine strips. • Peel the garlic cloves and the hardboiled eggs and dice both very finely. • Drain the pickles and dice very finely as well. • Wash the herbs, spin them dry and chop finely, chopping the chives into little rolls. • Mix all these ingredients into the cream, taste for seasoning and adjust. • Heat the waffle-iron according to instructions, grease with oil and bake crisp waffles with the dough. Serve as soon as possible with the herb cream.

Zucchini Flan with Lamb

Cut into 12 pieces

340 calories

Preparation time: about 45 minutes

Baking time: about 35 minutes

For the pastry:

1½ cups wholewheat flour, freshly ground

½ cup rye, finely ground

½ cup sesame seeds

1 tsp. baking powder

1 egg

1 cup creamy plain yogurt

Pinch salt

¼ tsp. dried thyme

3 tbs. olive oil

For the filling:

1 red pepper

2 onions

2 cloves garlic

3 ripe large tomatoes (1½ lbs.)

5 medium-size zucchini (1 lb. 2 oz.)

4 tbs. olive oil

10 oz. ground lamb

Salt

Black pepper, freshly ground

Cayenne pepper

1 tsp. fresh thyme leaves

½ tsp. fresh oregano leaves

½ a lemon

Olive oil for greasing and pouring

1⅓ cups mozzarella cheese

2 tbs. sesame seeds

For the pastry mix the wheat and rye flour in a bowl with the sesame seeds and the baking powder. • Whisk the egg with the yogurt and stir into the flour mixture together with the salt, thyme and olive oil. • Leave the pastry to rest in the refrigerator while you get the filling ready. • For the filling, remove the stalk, membranes and seeds from the red pepper, wash it, and after drying cut into very fine strips. • Peel the onions and cut into rings, peel the garlic as well and dice very finely. • Scald the tomatoes with boiling water, cool them down quickly with cold water, skin and halve crossways. Remove the core and the seeds and chop the flesh very finely, almost into a pulp. • Wash the zucchini, dry, remove the stalks, flower, and slice. • Heat the oil gradually in a pan and fry the sliced zucchini, a few at a time. Remove the few you have just cooked before adding the next, and drain on paper towels. • Put the paprika strips and the onion rings in the pan and cook, stirring continuously, until transparent. • Now add the ground lamb and fry, continuing to stir, until it is grey and crumbly. • Add the garlic, together with the chopped tomatoes. Season everything with salt, pepper and cayenne pepper, and the herbs and simmer without a lid until almost all the liquid has evaporated. • Wash the lemon in hot water, grate off some rind and stir into the meat mixture, together with the extracted juice. • Take the pan off the heat and allow the mixture to cool somewhat. • Preheat the oven to 400°F. • Grease an 11 in. diameter spring-release pan with some oil, put in the pastry and smooth flat with a wet spoon. In between carefully fold the sliced zucchini into the meat mixture and spread this on the pastry. • Drain the mozzarella and cut into thin slices. Place in a layer over the filling, sprinkle with the sesame seeds and dribble some olive oil over it. • Place the pan on the lower shelf of the hot oven and bake for about 35 minutes until golden brown. • Allow the flan to steam off for a very short while. When it comes out of the oven, cut into pieces and then serve immediately.

Leek and Onion Flan with Nuts

6 pieces

845 calories per serving
Preparation time: about 45 minutes
Cooling time: about 30 minutes
Baking time: about 35 minutes

For the pastry:

2¼ cups wholewheat flour, freshly ground

1½ cups rye, finely ground

1 tsp. baking powder

Pinch salt

½ tsp. dried marjoram

2 cups ricotta

8 tbs. milk

1 egg

8 tbs. oil

For the filling:

2¼ cups onions

2 sticks leeks

¼ cup butter

2 cloves garlic

½ cup vegetable broth

2 tbs. lemon juice

Salt

White pepper, freshly ground

3 sprigs thyme

Cayenne pepper

½ cup cashews

4 eggs

cream

1¼ cups Emmental or old Gouda cheese, freshly grated

Oil for greasing and pouring

For the pastry, mix the wheat and rye flour with the baking powder, salt and grated marjoram. • Put the ricotta in a bowl, together with the milk, egg and oil, and beat together thoroughly, gradually adding about two thirds of the flour. • Put the rest of the flour mixture on a work surface, spread the ricotta mixture over it and knead everything thoroughly to a smooth dough. • Shape into a ball and allow to rest in the refrigerator for about 30 minutes, wrapped in plastic wrap. • In the meantime peel the onions and cut into rings for the filling. Clean and wash the leeks, and after draining cut into pieces about 2 cm long. • Heat the butter in a large frying-pan or saucepan and cook the onions in it, stirring continuously, until golden brown. Then add the leek pieces and fry as well until transparent. • Peel the garlic cloves, dice very finely and mix into the vegetables. Quench immediately with the vegetable broth and season with salt, pepper and the lemon juice. • Rinse the thyme, pat dry and remove the leaves. Put them into the onion mixture together with a hefty pinch of cayenne pepper, and let everything cook over a low heat, without a lid, until nearly all the liquid has evaporated. • Remove the pan from the heat and allow the mixture to cool slightly. • Preheat the oven to 400°F. In the meantime, chop the cashews roughly. • Whisk the eggs with the cream and half of the grated cheese, and season with salt, pepper and cayenne pepper. Grease a baking sheet with some oil and roll out the pastry onto it. • Mix the nuts and the rest of the cheese into the onion and leek mixture, and spread out onto the rolled-out pastry. • Pour the egg and cheese mixture over the leeks and onions and dribble some olive oil over it. • Place the sheet on the middle shelf of the hot oven and bake the flan for about 35 minutes, until light brown. • Remove from the oven add allow to cool. Cut into pieces and serve hot.

Vegetable Turnovers with Crab

Makes 10

315 calories
Preparation time: about 1½ hours
Cooling time: about 2 hours
Baking time: about 20 minutes

For the pastry:
1¾ cups wholewheat flour, freshly ground
½ cup green rye, finely ground
1 egg
1 tsp. soy sauce
Cayenne pepper
½ cup sour cream
¾ cup butter
For the filling:
½ cup tofu
3 tbs. soy sauce
2 tbs. dry sherry
1 clove garlic

1 small stick leek
2 sticks pale celery
¾ cup beansprouts
3 tbs. oil
Salt
White pepper, freshly ground
2 tbs. cream
Scant ¼ tsp. ground ginger
4 oz. shelled crab
Wheatflour for rolling out
1 egg yolk
2 tbs. milk
Butter for greasing

For the pastry, mix the wheat and green rye flour, put onto the work surface and make a well in the center. Put in the egg, together with the soy sauce, some cayenne pepper and the sour cream, and dot the butter, in small flakes, around the edge. • Knead all the ingredients very quickly to a smooth, soft dough,

shape into a ball, and place in the refrigerator, covered or wrapped in plastic wrap, for 2 hours. • Meanwhile, prepare the filling. Allow the tofu to drain and cut into strips about 1½ in. long, and ½ in. wide. • Stir together the soy sauce and the sherry. • Peel the garlic, push through the press into this mixture, and add the tofu. Allow it to draw in there for at least 30 minutes, turning several times. • Clean the leek, remove any very coarse leaves and halve the stick lengthways. Then wash thoroughly in cold water, pat thoroughly dry, and cut into strips about as thick as a matchstick. • Wash the celery as well, dry off and remove any possible hard fibers, starting at the root end. Then divide the sticks into small pieces. • Wash the beansprouts in a sieve in cold water, and allow to drain very thoroughly. •

Drain the tofu pieces similarly, retaining the fluid. • Heat the oil in a pan, brown the tofu on all sides, turning, and remove from the pan. • Put the leek and celery pieces into the pan and fry very quickly over a strong heat. • Mix in the beansprouts and pour on the retained liquid from the tofu immediately. • Stir in the salt, pepper, cream and ginger and bring everything to a boil. Add the crab and remove the pan from the heat immediately, so that the vegetables do not become too soft. • Preheat the oven to 400°F. • Roll out the pastry on a lightly floured surface to about 1½-2 in. thick, and cut out circles about 5 in. in diameter. Spread the filling onto these, leaving the edges clear. • Brush the edges with cold water, fold the pastry parcels over into half-moon shapes and press the edges together well. • Whisk the egg yolk with the milk, brush the turnovers with it and place them on a greased baking tray. Place this on the middle shelf of the hot oven and bake the turnovers for about 20 minutes until light brown. • Take the vegetable turnovers off the tray and serve immediately, as they taste best when warm.

Spicy Cheese Puffs

Makes 30

80 calories per serving

For the pastry:
½ cup almonds, very finely chopped
½ cup water
2 pinches salt
¼ cup butter
½ cup wholewheat flour, freshly ground
½ cup green rye, finely ground
3-4 eggs
1 tsp. paprika powder
½ cup grated Emmental cheese
Butter for greasing
Wheatflour for dusting
For the filling:
1¼ cup full fat cream cheese
1 cup cream
1 egg yolk
Salt
White pepper, freshly ground
Paprika powder
Cayenne pepper
2-3 tbs. gin
1 dash Worcestershire sauce
1 onion
2 bunches chives

Roast the almonds in a dry pan until they are pale yellow. • Bring the water to a boil in a saucepan, with the salt and butter. Shoot the two sorts of flour in at once, and continue to heat, beating, until the mixture forms a smooth ball and a pale skin on the base of the pan. • Put the pastry into a bowl and stir in immediately 1 egg, the paprika powder and the cheese. • Allow the pastry to cool down, and then gradually work in the rest of the eggs and the almonds. • Preheat the oven to 425°F. • Grease a baking tray, dust with flour and place little mounds of mixture about the size of a walnut on it, leaving space around them; bake for about 20 minutes on the middle shelf of the oven. • Then cut through horizontally and leave to cool on a wire rack. • Beat the cheese to a creamy mixture with the cream and the egg yolk, and season with salt, pepper, cayenne pepper, paprika powder, gin and Worcestershire sauce. • Peel and grate the onion. • Wash the chives, pat dry and cut into little rolls. Stir into the cheese mixture with the onion and fill the cheese puffs with it.

Index